Stocks Re-visited

Peat-cutting

By the same author:
THE LOST VILLAGE OF STOCKS-IN-BOWLAND
LANCASHIRE WITCH COUNTRY
BOWLAND AND PENDLE HILL
LANCASHIRE MILLTOWN TRADITIONS
PENNINE BIRDS (with Bill Robson)

Stocks Re-visited

More Tales of a Lost Village in Bowland

Catlow Farmhouse

by W R Mitchell

Drawings by Peter Fox

CASTLEBERG
1993

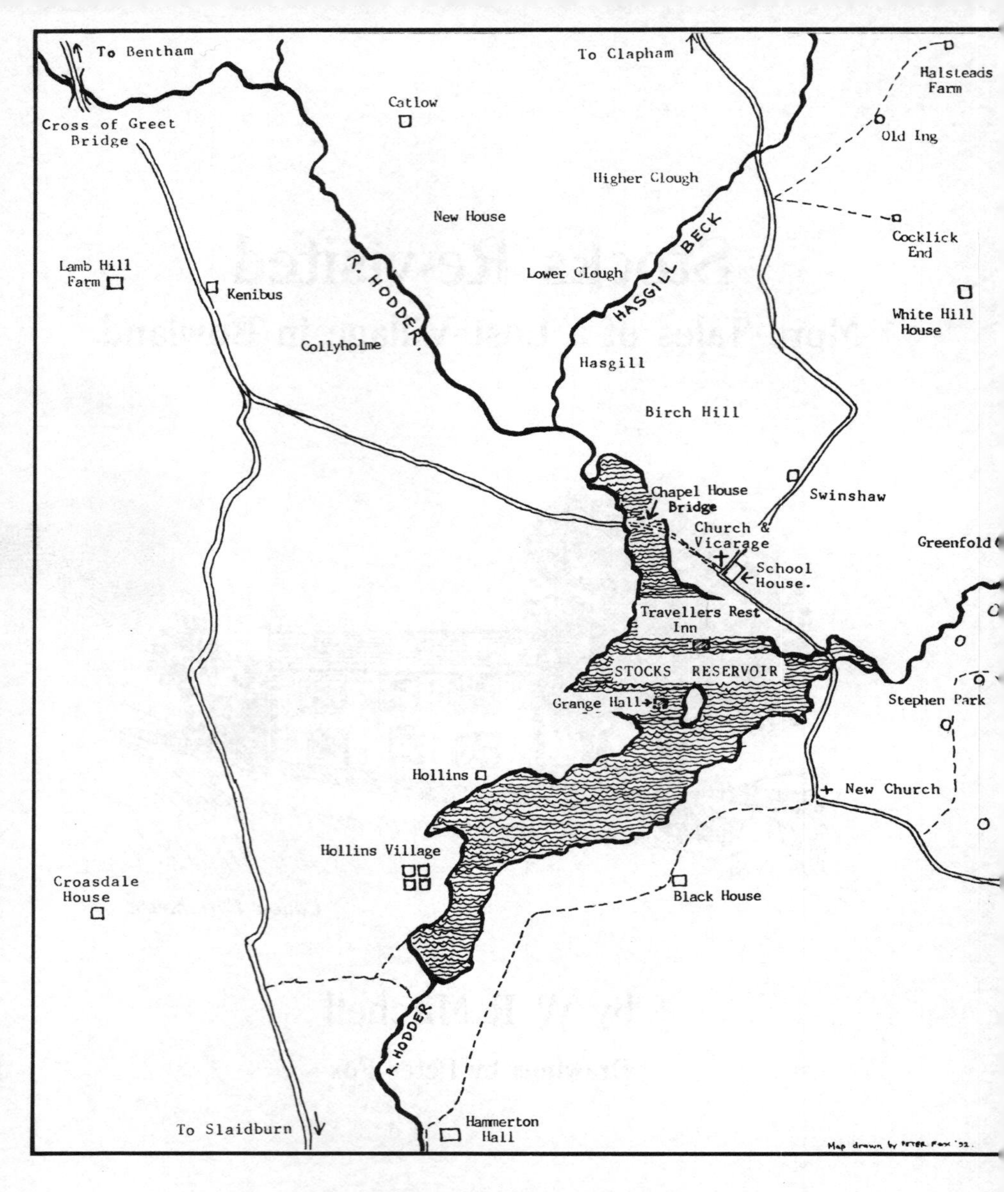

Published by Castleberg, 18 Yealand Avenue, Giggleswick,
Settle, North Yorkshire, BD24 0AY

Typeset in Clearface and printed by Lamberts Printers,
Station Road, Settle, North Yorkshire, BD24 9AA

ISBN: 1 871064 96 1

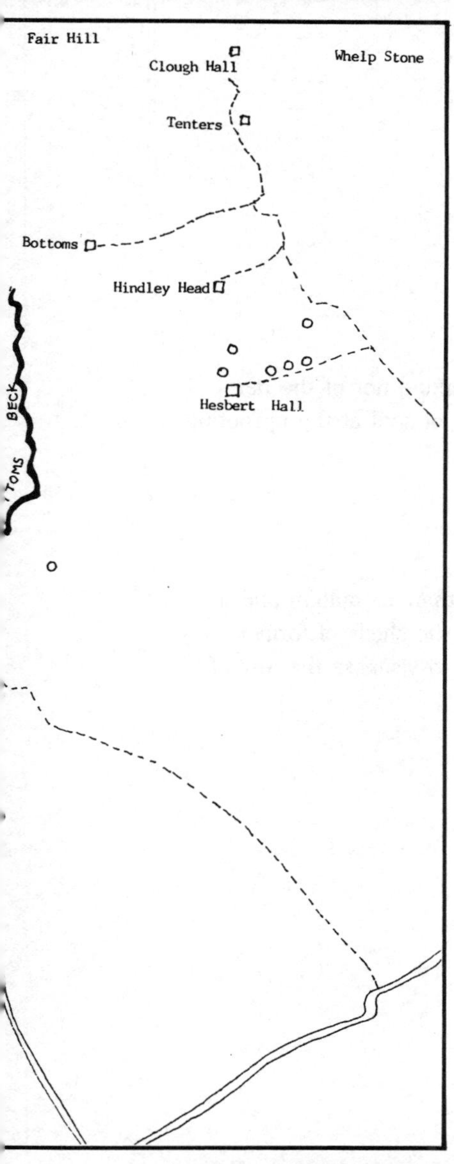

Contents

Acknowledgements

John Barry, Clitheroe Advertiser, Clitheroe Reference Library, Violet Cowgill, Tom Cowking, Bill Harrison, Mrs Mary Jolly, Doris Leeming, Tom Lodge, Eva Robinson, George Robinson, Vic Robinson, Eleanor Sedgwick, Percy Tilbury, Robin Waddington, Doris Wells, J S Walker, David and Julia Wood.

We were a happy community...

John Walmsley, of Stocks Fold.

The majority of the people have gone, thinking not of the new Dalehead but of the old. They are bruised of soul at the uprooting of much they held dear.

Advertiser and Times, July, 1932.

Blackpool got its water at a cost of more than £3 million and a community had been destroyed...Even if the shells of former farmsteads were located, it would be hard to visualise the way of life sixty to seventy years ago...

Horace Cook (1975).

A Forest Never Sleeps

ON MY first visit to Bowland, forty years ago, I chatted with a farmer at a hill farm near Slaidburn and had an insight into local pride in belonging to this glorious region of quiet dales and rounded fells.

I mentioned Bowland. He snapped: "It's Bolland, lad." I referred to Lancashire. He suggested I should wash my mouth out with carbolic soap. The smile on his face took the sting out of his words.

I began visiting the upper valley of the Hodder, in the wild west of Yorkshire, to watch birds and beasts. Mature indigenous timber clung to the sides of the valley down which Bottoms Beck coursed to give Stocks Reservoir an infusion of cold water. The battalions of sitka spruce, planted on the catchment of that man-made lake, were as yet like a thin stubble on the landscape.

It was an exciting time in the Forest of Gisburn, a name being used by the Forestry Commission. Short-eared owls—like big brown moths—quartered the ground for voles. At dawn, in early spring, black grouse displayed to each other in pairs, drooping their wings, stretching out their their necks, inflating their red wattles, coo-ing and periodically giving what sounded like a sneeze. The blackcock which held the best ground mated with the visiting greyhens.

Much later, when the trees had "takken 'od", blocking out half the sky—and when the black grouse had to do their cooing and hissing elsewhere—I discovered that the forest held sika, an astonishing species of deer—one which communicated by whistling and, when agitated, spread its white tail hair until it resembled a powder-puff and bounced along as though it had springs on its feet.

This Yorkshire forest (as it was until the insensitive boundary changes of 1974) extended from the Rocking Stone on Giggleswick Common to near Halsteads Farm and southwards to the Dalehead road. A tedious blanket of sitka spruce was relieved by a gridiron of "rides" where, in the absence of sheep, even the meanest flowers had a chance to realise their full potential. Thistles were the size of shrubs. Grasses rose to the height of the proverbial elephant's eye. In a limestone area, I found birds-eye primrose and orchids.

A friend who worked for Fylde Water Board gave me a boat ride to the island in the reservoir. We landed to the squawking of hundreds of nesting black-headed gulls and came under the unblinking gaze of a Canada goose sitting so tightly on her nest, she resembled a feathered tea cosy.

As I sat at the rim of Whelpstone Crag, surveying my domain—for there was never anyone about to challenge my unwritten claim to the land—I saw the roofs of farmsteads and outbarns breaking the monotony of dark green needles. That was long before the Forestry Commission deterred trespassing by the drastic action of blowing up the houses.

Some derelict buildings were tenanted by barn owls. In the evening, from a hiding place among the trees, I would glance across a sunlit glade, where clouds of midges danced, to where a shining white owl stood on the ledge of a forking hole and was stimulated to hunt for voles by the hunger-calls of its unseen young. Their rhythmic hissing was akin to snoring. On a warm evening, I had to fight to stay awake!

One newly-fledged family of owlets undertook their first flight—directly on to the roof of the hide in which I was sitting. I was keeping a note of owlish behaviour for a naturalist friend, Derek Bunn.

The claws of those young owls penetrated the hessian not more than a foot above my head.

Having become a freeman of the forest (complete with Forestry Commission permit) I began to study old farms and the reservoir-building days of not-so-long-ago. An sika stag was fond of lying on part of the old rail track, now swaddled in trees. Who had put a railway through this unpromising terrain?

Bottoms Farm still held one of the old iron fireplaces, complete with water boiler and oven, which featured in so many memories of th'owd uns I had met on my Bowland travels. Extending from Hindley Head, among the upstart spruce, was a line of magnificent beeches. Northfield, now a ruin under Whelpstone Crag, was typical of those on the higher land, being mainly tewit-land [the nesting place of lapwings] and "more or less all bent grass—not so very good." Tom Lodge mentioned the limited meadowland. "Dad had a horse and a mowing machine and a family to throw things about."

Poking about among the relics of a lost community, I pondered on the former pastoral life, when no one had heard of the Fylde Water Board, much less its plans to flood the valley and connect the reservoir with the taps of Blackpool and Fleetwood.

I became friendly with Percy Tilbury, his wife and children—the Children of the New Forest—who lived what to many townsfolk would appear to be an idyllic life at a home surrounded by fields behind a lack lustre screen of conifers. Percy worked for the Forestry Commission and also had the opportunity to indulge his love of farming.

From the yard outside Percy's home, I had glimpses of the changing seasons—the snow which subtly altered the contours of the landscape in winter and which, when melting, revealed the trackways of innumerable field voles; the leafing-up of the larch plantations in spring and their colonisation by sparrow-hawks;

summer days in the hayfield and autumn evenings, with the sun setting like a fireball beyond Stocks.

Autumn was my favourite season. As the day greyed into dusk, the first of the sika stags might be heard announcing its presence to the hinds by giving a sequence of three squeals. Each squeal rose and fell in a lovely crescent of sound. From a distance the sikine calls sounded like the pipes of a northern Pan.

Apart from Percy and his family, and the lone figure of Derek Bunn, I rarely saw another human being. Yet within living memory, Dalehead had been the home of several hundred people—men, women and their large families. I have already recorded some of their doings in *The Lost Village of Stocks-in-Bowland,* published at Christmastime, 1992. More about people and events at Dalehead in pre-reservoir days is now offered in *Stocks Re-visited.*

As before, I thank the Daleheaders who rummaged among the lockers of the mind and brought forth stories of the past. Without exception, they welcomed me to their homes. Sometimes I had to wait a while before a knock on the door was answered by a spirited but stiff-legged Daleheader operating a zimmer-frame.

Most of them are blessed with good memories. Tom Cowking mentioned the days when, each November, sheep were salved, having a mixture of tar and butter applied to their skins after the systematic "shedding" of the wool. Man and sheep sat on a stock. The salving bowl was of wood, with a long handle which thinned and could be pressed into a hole on the stock so that it would be handy.

I recall 89-year-old Alice Cowking holding up a birthday card on which a young friend had reproduced, by the latest computer technique, a photograph from her album, showing herself as a child in the arms of her mother. It is always a delight to chat with Robin Waddington who, born in 1907, still uses many of the old dialect words and expressions.

Robin told me about two old-fashioned ladies—Ellen and Jane Whipp—who lived at Stephen Moor at a time when farmers carted coal from Long Preston station. The two ladies were out walking. Some coal must have fallen from a cart because one of them had a large cob under her arm. "My mate, Harry Metcalfe, says to her: 'Is ta cartin' coyle fra Long Preston station?' Well, she put on a spurt and caught Harry in a plantation by the school. She did leather him."

He mentioned Mr Tuke, the blacksmith, who had two little lads, named David and Tommy. Once, when "clonking" David for a misdeed, he turned towards Tommy, who protested: "I've done nowt, father." Tuke retorted: "No—but thou will be doing afore neet."

Dalehead families were large and old-established. A common surname was Robinson, with branches of the family living at Catlow, Swinshaw, Stephen Park, Black House and Hesbert Hall. Vic Robinson's tales catch the spirit as well as the circumstances of t'old days. He was brought up at Stephen Park (which is still thankfully intact, being used as a field centre for schoolchildren). The family was large; men were employed and people were always popping in for a chat. Invariably they stayed for a meal. "Nobody went away hungry."

Quite often it was something with home-fed, home-cured bacon. The pigmeat might be seen hanging from hooks driven into the kitchen ceiling. Vic's father, Stephen, was also known to kill one or two wethers [male sheep] and sell the meat, operating with a horse and flat cart. The wethers selected for the knife were those inclined to stray. "If one or our sheep got the urge to wander, it was soon on to Hesbert Hall land and there was nothing to stop it travelling further—on to Fair Hill, Clapham Fell and down Keasden."

Strays were found in the periodical "gatherings" and returned to their owners. "If a stray was a wether, we used to put it inside and my dad [Stephen] killed it. He had succeeded his brother Tot [Tom] as the farmer at Stephen Park and also had a good little butchery business."

I heard tales about the Cowkings of Grange Hall; the Parkers of Colleyholme; the Carrs of Fair Hill, the Hansons of Bridge House and the Lord family who lived—where else, but Chapel House? Big families were the rule rather than the exception. Isabel Spencer, of Hawkswick, married John Lodge, who was born at Scar House, Buckden, and they farmed at Tenters and Northfield.

Isabel bore him ten children, losing the youngest child when he was aged eighteen months. Isabel died when she was only 34 years of age. Tom Lodge, one of that large family, told me: "There were nine of us. The youngest is seventy-five this year and we were all living up to last Christmas, when a brother died."

Two farmers, the Johnson brothers, who lived at Merrybent were on their own. One of them was a bootmaker. Eleanor Sedgwick recalls: "I did not know until I was walking up the Bentham road one Saturday and met him. He was going to deliver some boots at Bentham, so he would have to walk there and back."

Early this century, there was social stability. A harvest-tide hymn included a line about the rich man at his castle and the poor man at his gate. Few people were rich. The vast majority stood at their gates and did not envy. They had been brought up to respect their betters and, among themselves, they had no consciousness of being poor because all were "in t'same boat".

Farm work was labour-intensive. Irishmen, mainly from County Mayo, recruited at the hirings of Bentham, Bolton-by-Bowland, Clitheroe and Skipton, provided additional labour at haytime. Each bargain was sealed when the farmer handed over a shilling.

"That was supposed to be binding. . ." Tom Cowking's sentence ended with a laugh.

Just prior to 1914, the going rate for a month's labour was £4. If the work was done earlier, the Irishman could leave. If haytime was not over, the farmer had to re-negotiate terms—or the man was entitled to go elsewhere.

The first-named hiring took place at Bolton-by-Bowland on June 28. The Irishmen congregated at the *Coach and Horses.* Tom Cowking recalls: "If a farmer wanted a man, he usually brought a trap so that he could take him home or, with the promise of a higher wage, and shilling or no shilling, he'd probably not turn up.

The Irishmen, being Catholics, insisted on fish being served on a Friday. Tom remembers his aunt putting some meat on a plate. The Irishman said: "Oh Jasus, we don't ait mait on Fridays." The men from the Emerald Isle would walk down to the pub at Slaidburn or Newton and drink as much ale as their skins would hold. "And then they'd walk down to Dunsop Bridge to go to the Catholic Church."

Dalehead families were "heafed" like the sheep and, even when they moved away, they contrived to return periodically, to "leuk ower t'owd shop". Some returned regularly to Tosside, attending dances organised by Ellis and Elsie. Tom Cowking (who himself has played amplified music at hundreds of local dances) says: "As soon as Tosside hut was put up, dances went with a bang. People came from far and near. Ellis worked hard to get good bands. They left nothing to chance. He and his wife went to listen to the bands before they decided to give them a booking."

Says Mrs Cowking: "In our case, we went on bikes. The dance would be until two o'clock. Then they would have a whip round for the band and dance till three o'clock. Sometimes they had another whip round. In summer, we went home in daylight. After one Whitsuntide dance, when I was working for my uncle near

Holden, I got back just in time to change into my working clothes and bring the cows in to be milked."

It was a boon and a blessing when Isaac Bleazard, who had a haulage business at Bolton-by-Bowland, used one of the lorries to run people to Clitheroe (return fare: eightpence). He also went to dances at Tosside, when the fare was "a few coppers". Tom Cowking recalls: "In the 1920s, Isaac had a hen cabin fixed to a wagon and a step-ladder to go up into it. In the cabin were two forms—one up each side. We all crowded in."

John Hodgson, of Slaidburn, who had a haulage business, specialising in transporting lime, "went bankrupt" but started up, again, with a rudimentary bus service. He had contacted those to whom he owed money. Eventually, he paid them back—with interest.

A passenger on the Hodgson service had to climb a step ladder and he or she sat under a canvas hood. Tom Cowking says: "John Hodgson not only took passengers; if you asked him, he would bring you any goods you wanted, such as groceries." And lots of times, when the vehicle was unable to surmount Dunnow Hill, just out of Slaidburn, the passengers had to dismount and walk to the top. In 1921, Alice Cowking rode in "that contraption" to Preston to hear Dame Clara Butt.

Isaac Bleazard and John Hodgson eventually invested in buses. Isaac faced competition from the *Ribble* Company, who tried to drive him out, but he cunningly waited until the *Ribble* bus drove up to its stand at Clitheroe and then he would drive his bus in front. "He would be going out first, so people who were in a hurry got in his bus."

Daleheaders returned in droves to Dalehead Church for the Harvest Festival. Some of them returned for ever, having claimed a plot in the churchyard. Stephen Wood (1836-1911), of New House, spent his last years at Rylstone but his body was brought back to Dalehead for burial.

There was a resilience about anyone born and reared by the Upper Hodder. And the child-bearing capacity of the womenfolk was legendary, with the one branch of the Carr family having no less than fourteen children.

Mary Frankland Wood—known as Polly—while working at Swinshaw as a maid in 1890, had a son, David, who was baptised at Dalehead Church. Later, while working as a maid at Hasgill for James Johnson, Polly had a second son, Joe. Polly married Mr Johnson, when he was a good age and they had three children—Ellen, Mary and John—the father dying in 1900, aged 70 years.

The indefatigable Polly married Harry Pettiford and they moved to his home at Bridge House, Eldroth, where they had three children—Henry, Eva and Alice. Polly herself died in 1909. She was only 44 years of age.

Hearing about th'owd folk was always a humbling experience. They managed so well on so little. Sixty-three years ago, when Tom and Alice Cowking were married, they moved into a tiny cottage and all they possessed were the few bits and pieces bought in the sale of the lady who was leaving the cottage. Alice recalls that she left one object—a pot dog, which had a place of honour on the bedroom mantelshelf.

"This little dog—about six inches high—had its front paw but the back one had been broken off. You didn't notice this if you set it on the mantelshelf at a certain angle. I gave this little dog away to one of the family. I asked her the other day if she still had it. Oh, yes—it was treasured. I shouldn't wonder if that little dog was a hundred years old."

Ellen Taylor (nee Cowking), reared at Lamb Hill, married soon after the 1914-18 war and she and her husband had a lean time in the Slump. Prices dropped; all their capital was in stock. They reared calves and made a bit of butter, perhaps 12 lb a week at

1s.8d a lb. This, with a few dozen eggs, was virtually all the money that came into the house.

Living off the land was varied but the river Hodder offered them salmon. A visitor to Black House, one evening, saw young men congregating. "There would be five of them. They were going salmon poaching. They got away with it for quite a time and then they got a new water bailiff, who was a bit keener and there was some trouble."

The women were, in general, excellent cooks, as the food assembled for parish and church events testified. Drina Robinson, of Stephen Park, made the wedding cake for a Dalehead schoolteacher "and you could not have had a better cake. It had all the best ingredients and was beautifully iced. I wondered where she had learnt cake-making, but I must not have asked at the time."

The early 1930s were straitened times though, as Violet Cowgill (nee Tillotson) told me, there were joyful events such as the Stocks and District Farmers' Ball, held in the Cinema at the "shanty village" of Hollins in February, 1933. The proceeds went to Blackburn Infirmary. Violet's father was Chairman and John Walmsley of Black House Farm served as Secretary of the organising committee.

"I remember the weeks of preparation for the Ball. There were fruit cakes to bake and decorate; cutlery to mark with different coloured threads and crockery to unpack and wash." For the meal itself, thirty pounds of best beef was bought off Mr Ward, the butcher of King Lane, Clitheroe, at ten old pence a pound. "I saw it being lifted out of the fireside oven. That beef looked lush and appealing after the long, slow cooking.

"Mother made a cover for it, using flour and water, rolling it out and gently shaping it over the beef. All this was long before the days of aluminium foil. The last items to be made were dishes of trifle, with whipped cream."

The Tillotsons had a long friendship with the Cottams. Harry Cottam was the resident engineer from the beginning to the end of the scheme which turned Dalehead into a reservoir. Before marriage, Mrs Cottam had been an actress. She confessed to being glad to be clear of such a "bitchy" profession. As a militant supporter of "Votes for Women", she had been arrested, and imprisoned for a few hours for civil disobedience.

Mrs Cottam's mother, Mrs Fulshaw, lived in Persia but occasionally visited her daughter. Violet Cowgill recalls: "She was a lovely lady, kind and understanding. Her daughter was just like her." When Mr Cottam retired from the service of the Fylde Water Board, he and his wife settled in a house near the foot of Shap. Violet and her husband, Tom, called to see them on their way to Scotland in June, 1949. (The Cowgills, having saved up 36 petrol coupons, travelled nine hundred miles in Scotland for £3.10s.).

Mr Cottam—and no one thought of using his Christian name—periodically visited Slaidburn for a "crack" with his old friends and in August, 1949, was present when the fiftieth anniversary of the Fylde Water Board was celebrated "at the lower end of the reservoir". A marquee was erected and a cold buffet and drink provided.

Attending Slaidburn Show in 1957, he related to a friend that forty-seven years had elapsed since he first visited the valley. His grandmother visited Dalehead on foot in 1816. She called at the New Inn, Stocks Fold, for refreshment. While resting, she contrived to keep busy—by "footing a stocking".

She knew that the Devil had work for idle hands. It was a sentiment shared by the womenfolk of Dalehead. In winter, sometimes in the sitting room, the "pegging frames" would be brought out to re-cycle old clothes, using scraps in pegged rugs.

Life was chancy. A man who started work as a farm man says:

"I stopped wi' one chap for three year. When his family started getting up a bit, he remarked: "We can do wi'out you now." The farmers of Dalehead gloried in their independence and were as self-reliant as possible. They needed some of the town's goods, such as groceries and paraffin, contriving to pay for them on the barter system, using farm produce—butter, cheese and eggs.

Some of the larger firms in town sent their emissaries into Dalehead seeking orders for their goods. The orders were delivered a few days later by horse and cart. Dennis Byrne of Clitheroe supplied provvin [provender] and groceries, the orders being taken by a traveller called Harry Simpson. Once a week, Harry Taylor arrived at Dalehead to buy butter and eggs.

Among the drovers visiting Dalehead was Old Mick, the "bull-walloper", who lived at Settle. It was a drover's task to take farm stock to Hellifield auction mart. Mick became a celebrity, not as a drover but as a man who was reputed to be able to drink twelve pints of ale to twelve strokes of the clock. He had had a throat operation and could avoid the necessity to gulp. The achievement credited to him was impossible, of course, but he did well from the ale-money advanced by those putting him to the test.

The drover who collected "beeasts" from the Dalehead farms met up with his fellows, and other droves, at the lane end at the foot of Champions, on the road between Slaidburn and Tosside. By this time, the drove had swollen to a large size and the calling of cattle blended with the yapping of dogs and the shouts of the drovers.

Droving was not a highly-paid profession and the thirsty practitioners needed to be good scroungers. They could usually find a "bite and sup" somewhere or other and were happy if they could raise the price of a pint. Frank Dugdale wrote that the drover's life was made a little less "chancy" by the sale of whatever he could pick up for nowt—mushrooms, watercress, wild flowers and, when nobody was looking, rabbits or even a hare.

A drover who appeared before the local magistrates, charged with trespassing in pursuit of conies [rabbits], strenuously denied the charge. The chairman asked him where he had been going if he wasn't on the look out for rabbits. The rough old drover, his face softening, replied: "Primrosing, yer honour."

The Granary, Grange Hall Farm.

Some Dalehead Farms

They had big families and not a lot o' money.
Doris Wells.

You wouldn't gain anything with animals—cattle, sheep or pigs—if you bamboozled 'em about.
A Native of Dalehead.

OF THE farms of Dalehead, only five exceeded 200 acres, these being Stephen Park (355), Higher Halsteads (280), Fair Hill (464), New House (726) and Catlow (787). Many farms were little more than smallholdings. At Old Ing, Tom Taylor and his wife Lizzie had to be content with one pasture and one meadow. Neighbours often wondered how they managed to live and rear their four children.

As the reservoir work got under way in the 1920s, farms great and small were condemned to be vacated or demolished and the tenants dispersed locally—to Settle, Rimington, Skipton, Rathmell, Bolton-by-Bowland, Gargrave, Clitheroe, Tosside and Slaidburn.

By 1970, high explosives had been used in the demolition of farmhouses to absolve the Forestry Commission from possible claims for injury from incautious visitors. No one thought to record details of what they were about to destroy. Brown Hills had affinities with the old Norse longhouse, the living quarters and barn sharing a single capacious roof.

At Northfield, the explosion caused the four main walls to tumble inwards, with the roof falling neatly on top and the main chimney pot standing up, intact, on the heap of rubble. During demolition at Fair Hill, an ingenious double wall was located on the "weather" side. The total width was about six feet. Stephen Park and Hindley Head remain intact and are used by visiting school parties.

The following notes, gathered from local people, present the farms in alphabetical order:

Black House and Raingill

John Walmsley and his family returned to Black House after years spent in business at Stocks Fold. The farmhouse has survived, being well above high water mark.

John and his brother Tom told Frank Dugdale of their experiences during a winter at Black House when snow lay for weeks on end. The task of digging out snow and breaking up ice to permit the cattle to drink at the springs "nearly broke our backs and our hearts". Food for the poultry was brought from Hammerton Hall, yet many birds died.

Raingill, just down the field, also survives, with its conspicuous Welsh slate roof. Gamaliel and Mary Hanson had seven children.

Mary, a daughter, says: "Dad hated that name Gamaliel. He was nicknamed Gam or Maly."

A skilled joiner and able wheelwright, he augmented his income with woodwork. Among the jobs was repairing shelvings, a light frame made to fit over a cart so that its carrying capacity was increased. He also made hayrakes, having a special appliance for bending the bows. The Hanson sons did most of the farm work.

Mother devoted much of her daily round to butter-making, producing up to 100 lb of butter a week. She was also skilled at cheese-making. "My eldest sister, Laura, lived at Hasgill, having married Walter Brian (Wally) Blackwell, who when the reservoir work was in progress drove a locomotive and was photographed standing proudly beside the one named *Fylde*."

Bottoms Farm

Robin Waddington knew the Harrisons—Jonathan, Lizzie (Elizabeth) and their son Johnny. Mrs Harrison was "an off-cummed-un". They had a good farm, of about 120 acres, and they farmed it well. Jonathan, who was rather droll, used to say in his deep voice: "I could get some good lambs off it."

The Harrisons would never have left Bottoms if it had not been a "forced job". Let Robin continue the story: "When they were driven out of that valley—when t'Water Board got going and they had to flit—they came down to Brackenhurst. Th'owd folk were getting a bit old.

"Then from Brackenhurst, they took Weddicar at Gisburn. To get to it, you turn in just at t'side o' t'Commercial Hotel. I worked for 'em a bit. When it come spring end o' t'year, and they were thinking abaht flittin', I used to keep going off and on, taking part stuff."

Bridge House

At the time of the 1914-18 war, the Hansons lived at Bridge

House. When Heber Carr was called up into the Army, his wife [the Hansons' daughter] and their child, Ivy, moved into the farm for the duration.

Ivy recalls: "I had an uncle, Thomas Hanson, who lived quite near and who used to come and run the farm for my Grannie. There was also an auntie, 'Bel Hanson . . ."

Ivy has a special memory of the day when her father came home. "There was an old churn at Bridge House. Some churns went end-over-end, but this didn't. It was an older sort. When they churned, I used to sit on top of the churn. I was up there when my Dad arrived back. He was in uniform. I didn't know him . . ."

Catlow

The Robinsons have been at Catlow "a fair while". George Robinson told me that his father and grandfather, each named Thomas, farmed here, where the dale begins to give way to the rough grass leading to the watershed.

Being large and remote, Catlow had a strong appeal for the Clitheroe photographer, Buck, who recorded that in December 1923, the farmer noticed that his poultry were fretful. There must be a fox about. Shortly afterwards, near Bowland Knotts, the farmer saw a fox basking on a large stone. Believing that a disturbed fox makes uphill, he crept quietly round.

"Being too far off to kill, he fired a shot to see what happened. The fox jumped up from the stone and approached within twenty yards of where he was hiding. He fired again and stopped the career of Reynard. The farmer, impressed by the size and condition of the fox, had it "cured" and placed in a glass case "as an ornament for the sideboard and a token of the event."

Catlow Clipping was as renowned as that at Lamb Hill, drawing in voluntary helpers from a wide area. The dance which followed was, in the recollection of Doris Wells, a "country hop". Fiddle and concertina were popular instruments. Doris Wells remembers her father, Tom Carr, playing the concertina.

Chapel House

Buck, the ubiquitous photographer, visited Chapel House and took it for granted that the house had been a chapel, "as the walls show there have been alterations to the windows. One finds little chapels of this kind all over the district in out-of-the-way places, such as those of Tosside, Holden and Rodhill, and many more."

Buck presumed that such chapels were mainly a consequence of the Wesleyan movement; some were undoubtedly earlier. He mentioned Chapel House Bridge as being "the second that crosses the Hodder" and referred to "a lovers' walk through the plantation, at times carpeted with wild flowers. Also there is here a well of sulphur water. The trees on the banks come together and form a tunnel viewed from the bridge."

George Thompson remembers Chapel House as "a decent farm—it was down in the bottom."

Clough Head

Pronounce it "Cloo". Little of the farmstead remains. Before it was destroyed by explosives, a hole in the wall of the farmhouse had been a nesting place for a pair of redstarts.

Collyholme

It stands "straight down from New House, below Catlow, beside t'river." A footpath is indicated on the map. George Robinson recalls when there was a plank to enable people to cross dryshod in normal conditions.

Colleyholme, which was "not a bad farm", now goes with Catlow.

Robert Parker, who farmed the place at the edge of human memory, married twice. By the first wife, he had a daughter, Phoebe, and two sons, named Jack and George. Robert had "a boy and a girl by t'second wife."

Dob Dale

Meagre traces of this farm, together with an old ash tree, lie in the steep gill above the concrete bridge towards the head of the Forest. (Underneath the bridge, and some five feet ten inches above the normal flow of the beck, a forester painted a line to mark the height the water reached on August 20, 1967. The same storm devasted part of Wray, in the Lune Valley).

Fair Hill

Of all the "lost" farms of Dalehead, Fair Hill is the one that has the strongest appeal for me because of its wild situation. What remains of the place lies behind a belt of sitka spruce in a high, remote part of the forest.

The fell right at Fair Hill went on to Resting Stones [where the parish boundary met up with Lawkland and Giggleswick]. Doris's family, the Carrs, moved from Fair Hill to White Hill House, then Halsteads, from which—as a schoolgirl—Doris was sometimes prevailed upon to take letters left by Mr Swale the postman. He came to Dalehead three times a week—and did his best to avoid the long slog to Fair Hill.

When the Forestry Commission planted the ground, and the young trees were little more than a stubble on the landscape, it was still possible to visit Fair Hill and not too difficult to picture the farm life where a steep site had been levelled, using a substantial six foot retaining wall.

Nearby stand two outbuildings, one of which, with its double door, seems suited as a coach house and the other seemingly for the calves. Steps lead down beside the retaining wall into a garden, in a corner of which is a stone-built privvy. The big barn, shippon and baulks are further up the hill.

The demise of the farmhouse was in about 1970, when the Owners' Liability Act led to some of the old Dalehead buildings being demolished. Fair Hill was found to have an unusual feature, a double wall on the west with a total thickness approaching six feet. Some of the masonry was re-cycled, being used in a new bungalow.

In the Spring of 1993, when a competitive event for mountain bikes took in part of the Forest, the riders passed what remains of Fair Hill Farm and some selective brashing [thinning] of conifers opened up a direct path to the forestry road below. Fair Hill lost some of its sense of mystery.

William Carr, a native of Whitendale, married Elizabeth Robinson in 1878 and lived a short while at Birch Hill, then moved in 1880 to Fair Hill. It was in 1904 that Thomas, one of the Fair Hill twins, married Jane Harrison and went to White Hill House. Doris Wells, a daughter of Thomas, says: "I didn't come along till 1907. We moved up to Halsteads in the spring of 1910."

Eunice Carr, of Fair Hill, who became a maid at Catlow, married Mark Wood and they moved to a farm at Darwen, then back to Wigglesworth. Mark said of Darwen: "There were a lot of miners who had no respect for the land."

Fair Hill throbbed with young life in Edwardian times, when the Carr family consisted of William, Elizabeth Carr and their eight girls and six boys. The parents combined self-sufficiency with a moderate amount of bulk buying of provisions from the Settle tradesmen—28 lb of lard, 14 lb of currants and 1 cwt of sugar.

Every two days, up to eighteen pies and pasties were made and on baking day the oven held ten loaves at a time. The main fuel was peat, from a store replenished each summer, eighty loads of

Fair Hill.

peat being transported from Fair Hill Fell.

Fresh air and exercise, augmented by springtime doses of sulphur and treacle, kept the children healthy. In a case of serious illness, a horse was saddled for a crossing of Bowland Knotts to the doctor's house in Clapham.

Doris relates that when the children had grown up and dispersed, it was possible on only one occasion to assemble them for a family group. This occurred in 1908 or 1909 and a photographer was present to record the get-together.

Fair Hill was described by photographer E Buck as "the most outlandish farm in the dale." It was occupied by "another Robinson" when he called in the 1920s, and he recorded having a cup of tea and a good chat before setting off to cover the mile back to Halsteads.

Grange Hall

A grange was an outlying farm associated with a large monastic estate. This grange was owned by Kirkstall Abbey. The historian Whitaker noted that Grange Farm supplied the Abbey with loads of hay or straw. Miss Peel recorded that the farmstead as recalled was constructed in 1564 by the Russheton family, being first known as Rushton Grange.

Buck of Clitheroe was invited by Col Parker, of Browsholme, to meet him and W King-Wilkinson at Dalehead and they went to Grange Hall so that Buck might photograph it before its demolition.

Buck wrote: "To me, it seemed always to be a favourite place among the inhabitants. The Cowkings, who were the last tenants, seemed to be of a very genial and generous nature. . . It was a charming old place and our party was chiefly concerned with the carved masonry such as door lintels and windows of an ornamental nature, well worth preserving."

The photographer spent two days recording the building. "Before I had finished, the workmen were stumping the trees by the riverside and burning the rubbish so as to have the bottom of the reservoir clean. The Grange was next to come down and be cleared away." On another visit: "There was a void. . . What I had seen and knew very well had vanished like a dream."

As a farm, Grange was favoured by being on limestone, which outcropped here and also at Raingill, Slaidburn, Lane Ends and Bolton-by-Bowland. In the upper Hodder valley, Grange land was sweeter than that at the neighbouring farms. Tom Cowking says: "We used to move the lambs from Grange to New Close to give them a change from the limestone to the gritstone. They thrived better."

Tom also recalls a cow pasture of 60 acres or more. "We had a dog called Tidy. On a foggy morning, my Dad would send it to fetch the cows. It would go into the fog and bring them back, whether they were on the tops or down by the Hodder."

Of Grange Hall, he says: "There were really two buildings—Grange Hall and Old Hall, built endways on, but with no connection between the two through the interior walls. The upper room of the Old Hall was used as a dormitory for the Irishmen who helped with the hay harvest in July. We usually had four Irishmen at about £4 each per month.

"I remember when a lot of band instruments were stored in the upper room. I never knew who owned them. At ground level, there was a room used as a joiners' shop. The walls were nicely plastered, with cornices to the ceilings. The room had a wooden floor." Grange Farm was flanked by two lawns and a vegetable garden.

On the east side, a high wall—fifteen feet high at least—cheated the weather.

Photographs show a large outbuilding by the road. "The east end was used as a stable and trap house. The other end was usually used for butchering sheep. Tom's aunts and uncle used it as such before they moved to Nelson to open a butchers' shop. The old building was also in use when it was necessary to slaughter a sheep or two to augment the food supply at haytime.

Grange Farm stood near some famous stepping stones which enabled travellers to cross the Hodder dryshod. Tom says: "You had to be careful. Those river-washed stones could be slippery, especially in frost. And they weren't exactly level. If you were making some stepping stones today, you'd probably do them in concrete." When the river was in flood, the nearest crossing point was the bridge near the corn mill, a hundred yards away. "Then you had to go back through a meadow before you reached the stepping stones again."

The domed hill [which is now an island in the reservoir] was previously meadowland. Two meadows belonged to Grange Farm and one to Bridge House. Part of the land bore the mysterious name of Honeymouth, which previously had related to Honeymouth Mere, which was drained.

Tom Cowking's great grandfather, William, the first of the family to be associated with Grange Hall, made a corn mill to run off the Hodder. "The mill ground local corn until the American grain was being imported."

When Tom's father married, he left Grange Hall and went to New Close. "My Aunt Jane married and went to Hammerton Hall. An auntie and uncle, Belle and Titus, left for Nelson and started a butchery business. My uncle William married and went to Lamb Hill. Two maiden aunts, Betty and Bertha, kept house at Grange. They looked after the farm man and the summertime Irish helpers."

Tom Cowking was born at New Close but frequently visited Grange Hall. "It had changed over from a bucket pump to a pipe water supply just before my time. There was hardly any pressure; it was low gradient."

Tom has a vivid recollection of the interior. "You went through the front door into the passage, where the most important object was the barometer. My Aunt Betty used to tap it every dinnertime in haytime to see what the weather was going to be like."

From the passage, you entered the living kitchen, then the back kitchen. It was "a step down". Tom's aunts would be making cheese or butter. "Most of the cheese was produced in summer, when the farm had an extra staff, including the Irishmen. They ate more cheese to bread than they do nowadays. I remember one lady saying to the farm man: 'Are you going to eat some bread with your cheese, Bill?' He said: 'Anyone who can't eat cheese without bread deserves to clam [go in need]'."

Outside the building was a ponderous stone cheese press. Tom watched the milk being put into vats, and the rennet being added "to curdle it". Then the cheese was put in a press. "The stone of the press must have weighed a ton; you wound it up with a big screw and then lowered it on to the cheese box to press out all the whey. The cheese was dried on shelves in the dairy."

During summer, Tom's aunts brewed a very weak ale for the Irishmen. Uncle William—he who went to Lamb Hill—remembered when no one in the valley bought tea. "It was unknown until some of my aunties went away and, having had tea served wherever they visited, came back with some. We all gradually got on to it."

I asked Tom what happened in the parlour at Grange Hall. He replied: "Nothing much. It was Aunt Bertha's private place, more or less." The parlour had an ornate fireplace, with a mantelpiece covered with a cloth with a fancy fringe. Looking down from the mantelpiece were two pot dogs. "Everybody had pot dogs."

The table was covered with a tassled cloth. In the room was a horsehair sofa. "If you sat on that old, worn, horsehair sofa, it felt bristly." There was also a piano. "Aunt Bertha played for dancing and gave music lessons. In her spare time she painted Clitheroe Castle on double-yolked goose eggs for my sisters. When an egg was finished, she'd pass a ribbon through and put bows on each end. There'd be enough ribbon left to hang it up. It was quite a showpiece."

The Irish haytime men slept in an upstairs room, each man having a bed with a wooden frame and rope threaded round knobs attached to the side to provide a base for the mattress. "If the rope gave way, it was disastrous because it was without knots; the whole lot just sagged. The mattress was of rough cloth, packed with straw.

These men from Erin's Isle were not like Irishmen today. "They wore a lot of heavy clothes, with mufflers and long johns. The men employed at the Grange were well-fed. Everyone sat down at the same table. At some farms there was a distinction. The men ate separately." Tom remembers one or two farms at which the food for the hired men was somewhat inferior to that provided for the family. For example, sad cake, made with less lard than normal, was so hard "you had to break it over the table edge like cow cake."

Upstairs, the rooms were austerely furnished. "There were no luxuries then. No bathroom. No toilet—just chamber pots. I remember one person calling and Aunt Bertha saying: 'I bet he's never had a bath since his mother bath-ed him'."

Peat was cut on Bolland Knotts and the Grange Hall men went on to Lamb Hill Fell for brackens, needed for bedding the young stock in winter.

When Grange Farm was demolished, a special rail track was laid from the main line because a thick deposit of gravel was found under the farmhouse. "It went about eight feet below the foundations. So everything went into the bucket."

Halsteads

In 1910, the Carr family moved from White Hill House to Higher Halsteads, one of two farmhouses which were connected. Low Halsteads, an addition to the original building, was the home of the Dawsons—Tim (Stephen), Mary and their two daughters and a son.

At Higher Halsteads, the previous farmer, whose name was Paley, had come to an unhappy end while carting coal over the hill from Clapham station. Having sat on a shaft of the cart to attend to the brake as it was descending from Bowland Knotts, he slipped off and a cart wheel ran over him.

Doris Wells says: "Halsteads was really the best farm in the area; it had been well-farmed and, although I say it myself, my dad looked after it. This farm had stone walls, with very little fencing."

Tom Carr, of Halsteads, was "a terrible sheep man". He lambed over three hundred sheep. Robin Waddington remembers going to Halsteads with his father, who would buy about twenty sheep and drive them back to Middle Knotts Farm, two miles from Tosside.

Of the farmhouse itself, Doris remembers the blue flag floors, partly covered by pegged rugs. "My mother never had a bought rug or a bought carpet." One of the bedrooms had been partitioned. The one in which the girls slept had a window into the passage; there was no view of the outside world. "In summertime, that room used to get very warm."

Halsteads Farm.

Both farms at Halstead joined at the moor; there was no dividing fence. "The turf [peat] was coal-black and, when dry, became so hard it could hardly be broken." The Dawson family cut their peat at the other end of the moor and it was brown and fuzzy. "You wouldn't have thought there'd be so much difference in one piece of ground."

The High Halstead outbarn, being at the top of a hill, was not easy of access. In haytime, when hay was to be taken to the barn, a trace-horse was needed on the cart. "There were two shippons for six cows; that was twelve in all. The middle-aged stock was kept up there."

Hasgill

When it was a farm, long years ago, the potters camped every year beside the Clapham road. William Brown, of Hasgill, eventually married one of the gipsy girls.

One who knew her reports: "She was a grand woman and clean, with a herbal remedy for nearly everything." In summer, she'd gather different herbs and dry them. Many people went to her for help. "Course, they weren't daft, weren't gipsies."

Wally (Walter) Blackwell lived at Hasgill with his wife, Lois (a Carr, who had become his first wife). Wally was an engine driver for the Fylde Water Board. The farmhouse subsequently became a ruin.

Hesbert Hall

Three farms occupy this well-watered hillside site; they were all occupied up to the time of the Fylde Water Board and now there is but one family in occupation.

No one is sure which is the farm known as Hesbert Hall. The one tenanted today was once occupied by a family called Tenby "off Bentham side". Harry Jackson lived at the lower of the two remaining houses, outside which was a fine example of a lilac tree. "I don't know why or how but it always seemed to be in flower at Whitsuntide."

Harry used to repair clogs. "If you split your clog, you had to go after school, in the evening. Mother would say: 'You'd better tak that on to Hesbert Hall and get it mended'. You sat and waited till he had repaired it."

The higher farm was occupied by George Court, whose wife was a Harrison, related to Jonathan Harrison at Bottoms Farm.

Hindley Head

The farmstead remains almost complete, a short distance from Bailey Lane, having been adapted for use as a field centre for a school. Although the area was planted with spruce trees, there still remains a line of beeches on a bank which in the old days would provide bield [shelter]. The beech trees had been so sited, with regard to location and terrain, that they have been able to grow to an impressive size.

Thomas Wood, who was born at Newhouse in 1867, worked here with his father until his marriage to Mary Blackwell Brown, of Higher Clough at Dalehead Church in 1892.

They had three children. Mary (Polly) married Ned Marsden, who eventually worked on Stocks Reservoir and played in the Stocks Football Team. Tragedy befell the other two children, the second child dying in infancy and their third child being buried at Dalehead, aged six weeks, just four days after Mary herself was interred there.

Thomas then married Mary Harrison of Hindley Head; they had eight children and eventually moved to Eldroth and later to Draughton, between Skipton and Ilkley.

Lamb Hill

Col. Hirst had the shooting and he renovated the farmhouse, so that although it was basically old it has a modern appearance. Tom Cowking's uncle, William, was the bailiff here.

Lamb Hill Clipping was famous. Copious quantities of beer were consumed. "The clippers got a bit tipsy towards night. Then everybody went into the farmhouses for a hot meal—roast beef and 'all the trimmings', pudding and ale, though some settled for tea."

We know a good deal about Lamb Hill early this century through a record left by Ellen Mary (Nellie), daughter of William Cowking, who married a Taylor. Her "Lancashire Life Story" was a prizewinning feature in *The Farmer's Guardian* in 1948.

She wrote of lambing time and how, sometimes, if the ewes had little milk, she helped to bottle-feed lambs with cow's milk until eleven at night. "One horrible year, I remember, we buried eighty lambs in one grave. The ewes were in a very bad way, too..."

Then came the sheep-shearing. Lamb Hill Clipping took place about the middle of July. The sheep were first washed, a beck being dammed to form a "dub". The sheep were dropped in, one by one, and a man who stood waist deep in water ruffled their wool to remove traces of grit from the moors, plus the salve which had been put on the previous November so that the sheep might winter better. (A fleece from a washed sheep was worth more than one that remained unwashed, though the removal of grit and other impurities meant that its weight was reduced).

Ellen recorded how the boys helped to catch the sheep and take them to the clippers; when the shearing was over, boys wrapped up the fleeces. "My father and I would take jugs of beer around. It was a thirsty job, and we saw that they did not go short of anything, for all this work was done for nothing."

Ellen's special mission was enacted in the farmhouse kitchen, where she helped to pack food into the butter-baskets—sandwiches, freshly-baked pies and custards, pastry and cake. Jugs of tea were "mashed", the pots being kept in another basket. "Then we would wind our way up through the sheep-pens to the men."

When, that evening, the clipping was completed and all the helpers had washed, a good dinner was provided. "We had roast beef, legs of mutton, rabbit pies, mint sauce, onions and cucumber sliced up in vinegar, new potatoes (with plenty of butter on), peas, etc; apple tarts, gooseberry tarts, all made with puff pastry crust (my mother was a good cook), plum puddings with rum sauce."

The older men, retiring into the kitchen, sang songs, becoming quite merry as they sipped gin and whisky. "Most of the sweethearts and wives would be asked to the dinner, and afterwards the young ones would go into the loft, as we called it, and dance to the fiddles and concertinas—all played by ear. The popular dances were quadrilles, lancers, swing-six, schottische, polka and varsovienne."

Ellen, still a young girl, used to sneak up to the loft to watch. Her mother soon missed her and made her go to bed. "She was very strict with me."

Mr Buck, the photographer, had witnessed the Lamb Hill Clipping, where "there is great competition among the young as to who can clip most sheep in a given time. The farmers' wives and also the children are there to help and provide for the men who are to do the shearing."

There was great rejoicing when all the sheep had been clipped. A good supper was prepared in the barn. "Afterwards, dancing takes place till the small hours of next day, when they may be seen tired and making their way home across the fields with the satisfaction of something attempted, something done."

Having a lot of wool was no guarantee of prosperity in the pre-1914 period, when trade was bad. One proud Dalehead farmer would not sell the wool at a low price, so a five years' clip accumulated. The wool merchant came and saw it all weighed. He stayed a night or two. Will Cowking said: "I'll bet tha'll sell it all for new wool." The merchant replied: "Wouldn't tha?" The wool was sold for thruppence a pound.

Ellen was paid twelve guineas a year for her domestic efforts. When she "came of age" she went to another farm, for ten shillings a week, her work being mostly in the house. "I spent very little; my father's way was to save as much as possible. It was a good way, too. No pictures or amusements in those days—only tea-drinking at a friend's house."

During the 1914-18 war, her brother joined up so Ellen took his

place at Lamb Hill, "cleaning the shippons, milking and helping with the sheep. Once I went to do a bit of muck-spreading, but found the job much harder than it looked. "I used to mow with the machine and load the hay on to the cart and stack it in the barn, which is very hard work for a woman. Indeed, I worked like a man for the sum of sixteen shillings a week."

New Close

This farm is "out o' water—straight up from Grange Farm." Charlie Cowking and his family lived at New Close.

Tom Cowking recalls: "It was an up-to-date farmhouse, built in 1872—the only farmhouse I had seen with an overhanging roof. It came out about four feet from the walls and was lath and plastered. This was probably a mistake because plaster started dropping off and the birds got in."

The farmhouse also had a piped water supply and a smart approach, on concrete paths. "You went in at the front door and saw a staircase leading upstairs. The farm had parlour, kitchen with a bakestone [pronounced backst'n] for making oatcake. There was an outside wash-house. "Upstairs, the best room was over the parlour. Another big room in front and a passage to a back room—a cold room where the lads slept."

Like other Dalehead farms, the main fuel was peat. "We used to get our peats on Bolland Knotts," recalls Tom Cowking. "We took the implements up by horse and cart. The peat barrow had a big, broad wheel in front. We went backwards and forwards on bikes, day after day, laying out the peats, turning them, setting them up and then stacking them. We would cart peat back to the farm before haytime, if it was fit. It was quite a job."

The farm is no more. "The railway to Jumbles Quarry ran near it so they thought they'd pull it down and take the stone away and use it for the dam."

New House

New House stood "straight up from the reservoir, on the way to Catlow." To this farm, in the late 1880s, came the Wood family, who had recently been in the Bolton and Chorley area of Lancashire. David Wood, who was born in 1800, became a farmer and married Mary Harrison from Hindley Head on December 18, 1830.

One of their sons, Stephen (b.1836) married Mary Frankland, daughter of Thomas Frankland from Catlow on New Year's Day, 1861. They moved away into Lancashire and then moved back to "Newhouse" at Dalehead. It is said they arrived with their ten children and all their belongings on one cart. Jennie Wood, a surviving granddaughter of Stephen and Mary, says that he moved "so that his sons did not marry the worldly girls of Chorley."

Stephen reared sheep at New House, as testified by the sheep marks record of 1896. The family remained at New House until March, 1900 when Stephen moved to Rylstone. The Woods appear to have played a leading part in local Church life, for on their departure from Dalehead they were presented with a hand-painted plaque by the Vicar and parishioners.

George Robinson recalls that New House had seven bedrooms upstairs; downstairs was a living room, parlour, another room, two kitchens, one for living in and the other having a slopstone [stone sink] with a cold water tap, the water being conveyed through lead pipes from a spring in a nearby field. In this second kitchen was a set-pot for heating water, used for washing clothes. New House had a pantry, washhouse and a big cellar.

The main kitchen held an oak kist in which flour was stored. The flour was purchased in large bags made of well-bleached cotton. George Robinson recalls that "we used the bags to make brats [aprons]." Another basic commodity was pin-head oatmeal for

Continue on page 49.

Grange Hall Before the Flood

The monks of Kirkstall had the grange, which stood on a gravel bed to the west of what is now an island in the reservoir. Below: this postcard, from one of Mr Buck's photographs, was also used as a shopping list.

Transport Old and New

Above: a well-decorated working horse. Below: officials of the Fylde Water Board cause a sensation by driving a car to Stocks Fold in 1919.

Work and Pleasure

Above: Inlet end of the tunnel with steam crane.
Below: Stocks Football team of 1924: Front row (left to right): Joseph Green, R Atkinson and A Pinch. Second row: W B Blackwell, E Redfern, John Green, J Wilkinson (capt), J Whittaker, J T Tivey and J B Driver. Back row: R Wallbank, H Cottam (chairman), J Holden, G E Hirst, F Green, C Whitehead and G F Jeffs (league secy).

Above the Door at Stephen Park

The seventeenth century lettering forms the words "He that doth pass must Honest be: Not to Bold for You See." Stephen Park is now an outdoor centre visited by schoolchildren.

At the Edge of the Moor

Above: Lamb Hill, an old farm improved by the sporting Col. Hirst and the setting for a major sheep clipping which ended with food and dancing.
Below: womenfolk at Catlow on clipping day.

The Old Church at Dalehead

Dedicated to St James, it stood beside the road from Four Lane Ends to Bowland Knotts and had seating for 150 worshippers.
Below: Sports Day, with the Church as a backdrop.

Two Photographic Occasions

Above: Autumn, 1931, by the gates of Daleshead Church. The Rev Cyril Slater (last vicar of the parish), H P Killick (headmaster), Mrs Killick (in front of her husband), Mrs L Pickles (infants teacher).
Below: one of the many school photographs.

Iron Horse at Dalehead

Wally (Walter Brian) Blackwell and the steam locomotive “Fylde” during the construction of Stocks Reservoir. Stone for the dam was conveyed by rail from Jumbles Quarry. Equipment was railborne from a depot at Tosside.

porridge. "We bought this in 140 pound bags, same as flour. We never missed having porridge for breakfast." George smiled, adding: "I still do." Sugar was bought in hundredweight lots from one of the grocery firms such as Byrnes, of Clitheroe.

The floor of the living kitchen was covered with blue flags from Helwith Bridge. "Some of the slates would be two or three inches thick." They were regularly scrubbed, the scrubbers going down on their hands and knees. A "donkey stone" was used to give the edges a bright appearance.

Despite the hard work, a family developed a strong affection for the old farmstead. It also worked in reverse. Thomas Robinson, of New House, who married Ellen Taylor of Kirkby Malham, kept up the link with Malhamdale in that their four children were christened there. George was the eldest, followed by William, Thomas and Phoebe (who died when she was twenty-two years old).

The children had nearly two miles to walk to Dalehead school.

Stephen Park

Vic Robinson says: "There had been a Robinson for years at Stephen Park. . . Our landlord, Billy Procter of Kirkby Malham, once said that as long as there was a Robinson left, he had to have the farm."

Photographer Buck, having been asked to call at Stephen Park by Mrs Robinson, the farmer's wife, noticed "a peculiar doorway with an inscription in raised letters on the lintel stone. I learned it was formerly the front of the house, open to anyone passing. The other parts had been built in front, so that it is now the entrance lobby. Through this door was the parlour or best room."

Buck, anxious to photograph the inscription, though it was in a dark cramped lobby, gave the plate an exposure of three minutes and the photograph was successful. All the letters are joined up without any break, as follows:

HETHATDOTHPASEMUSTHONEST
BENOTTOBOLDFOREYOUSEE
HmBSE I 1662

Buck titled the inscription: "A silent sermon in stone."

Swinshaw

This farmhouse, recalls Doris Wells, was four-square with "a lovely garden . . . always some flowers, especially white rock.

"You went through the front door into a passage from which rooms went off."

The farmer, Stephen Robinson (commonly known as Tim), died young. He left a widow, Mary, and nine children—Dick, Tom, Fred, Charlie, Turner [after his mother's maiden name], Nancy, Frank, Isabel [usually called Bel] and Matt. "And do you know, they're all dead."

The mother is recalled as a plumpish woman. "They didn't diet in those days. And they produced big families. My husband used to say of a hefty person that he or she wanted girthing up."

Doris says: "On schooldays, we'd walk up to Swinshaw at dinnertime. We'd sit down in the living room and keep quiet while the Swinsto children had their dinner. Mother had given us jam butts [sandwiches]. They had their dinner, sitting on forms at the big deal table. There was a pint pot full of water in the middle of the table and they all drank from it.

Inside Swinshaw there was nothing fancy—not even rugs on the flagged floor." In the kitchen was a churn and an old-fashioned mangle. A wooden kist [chest] held food for the farm stock. The kist was kept scrubbed and used as a worktop. The sitting room, like many another, was virtually unfurnished. "The kids were in there if the weather was wet."

In the farmyard, at the top side of the house, a carthouse was "kept swept up and tidy" and on Thursday families gathered here with their butter and eggs for the dealers such as Harry Taylor of Holden. He was a dapper little man with a moustache. He brought apples and onions.

"The butcher came on a Thursday; if we were not there to collect our meat, Mrs Robinson would take it in. We were provided with a wooden butter box. It held about forty pounds. There were egg boxes, too, made of wood with cardboard sections within. Otherwise, an ordinary box was used, the eggs being packed in hay or straw.

Food and Water

It's yer stomach 'at 'ods your back up.
Dales saying.

You needed a lot o' fat then; in those days it was a matter of who had t'heaviest pig.
George Robinson.

FARM COOKING—a concept which modern advertising men use to signify the best of food—was somewhat varied at Dalehead. Doris Wells says that the diet was plain.

She remembers when a meal might incline sad cake, jam pasty and cheese, with fruit pies (gooseberry a favourite) in season. "Sad cake was made of pastry," she says. "You either put currants in it and made it something like an Eccles cake—though you were sparing with the fruit—or you just rolled it out as pastry: three pounds of flour to one pound of lard. People today are inclined to put too much fat in pastry."

Then there was "crackling"—not, in this case, the crunchy bit of pork but a refined sort of sad cake. "If mother had a bit o' pastry left on baking day, she'd roll it out thin, cut it into squares and bake it in a tin."

Farms were originally built where a good water supply existed. At Stephen Park, says Vic Robinson, "we had a pump on the right hand side of the porch as you went in; the water came through a lead pipe from a fourteen foot deep well. We also took water off the roof and stored it in a big tank for washing.

"There was a good spring in the back meadow. When the water we pumped up was not just up to standard, we bucketed water from that spring. It was one of the finest springs and it's running to this day."

George Robinson recalls: "The evening meal at the farm was usually a big one. It consisted of anything that was going—boiled ham or something like that. A lot of the food you ate was your own produce. For pudding, you had rice, barley or bread pudding. As a treat, there'd be jam roly poly [a suet pudding]."

Tom Cowking tells of two men who lived at a place near Lane Ends, Bolton-by-Bowland. One of them said: "We had stoated rabbits [freshly killed by a stoat and bled] and any old hen which had tummelled [fallen] off a perch. We were glad to get away."

Rabbit was a stable food. "There was a rabbit warren not far from New Close. Dad used to invite a few friends to a shoot. We had an old tortoiseshell cat. I used to follow it to the warren when I was just a kid. That cat would sit at the mouth of the hole. Young rabbits would come out to play. That cat never blinked an eyelid.

"All at once, it would lunge forward and get a rabbit, carrying it home in its mouth. When it got home, it went up the ivy. We didn't know what was going on up there till we saw some kittens walking on the ridge. Were they wild; they'd just sit and spit at you."

Baking day at Grange Hall, in the memory of Tom Cowking, involved the "hot air oven", which was about mantelpiece height. "Everything was baked in big tins. At haytime, there was all this extra staff. I remember potato pies in big square dishes, pudding and pastries and whatever. The flour and oatmeal were bought by the hundredweight."

Butter-making was a regular task on the farms of Dalehead. None of the milk went away as milk. The cream was separated, using a metal tray called a lead [pronounced led] and the blue milk fed to the young stock. Tom Cowking says: "We had to get our cream down from New Close to Grange Farm to be churned by the farm man. It was a paddle-churn. The farm man, a bit of an expert, went at a furious rate and it usually came to butter sooner than most churns did.

"My Aunt Betty supervised the churning; she scraped the inner part of the churn with a celluloid patch so that all the cream was churned. When it was butter, Aunt Betty worked it into round pounds. She had an old-fashioned English penny to put on the scale along with the pound weight. She made sure there was no short measure.

"Then the butter was taken away by one of the visiting factors. On Thursday, Stocks had a little market and the factors came to collect the products of the farms—butter, cheese, eggs, rabbits. Butter was retailed mainly in the Colne Valley. But first they mixed it with Keil (German or Dutch) butter. Each farm produced butter with an individual taste and the factors blended it to create a uniform taste. Otherwise, there might be complaints about the 'peculiar' taste which had been caused by a particular herb common on a certain farm."

Mary Jolly (nee Hanson) remembers, from her young days at Raingill, when cream was separated from the milk by allowing the milk to stand in a "lead" [a relatively shallow container, originally made of lead but latterly of a galvanised material]. A plug was withdrawn to let the "blue" milk drain away, and the cream was scraped from the sides.

Her mother produced 100 lb of butter a week. "At a busy time, she would make a hundredweight of butter." The butter was mainly in "round pounds", each with the outline of a cow stamped on it, using a stamp made of sycamore, because this did not taint the produce. "If the butter would not set during a hot spell of weather in summer, it was placed in basins."

Father took the butter to Clitheroe in the family car. "If he could sell it all, we had to have Danish butter; it was cheaper." Dad had many orders. Butter was never brought back to the farm, the surplus being taken to Boothmans, the grocers. When mother made cheese, of the Lancashire variety, the last of the whey was removed by pressing, using a big iron press."

Pigs were to be found at almost every farm. George Robinson says: "We usually had two, sometimes three pigs. We reared 'em from piglets—they were 'appen three months old. I liked pigs. I didn't like to see 'em killed when I'd fed 'em and made a bit of a fuss of 'em."

Pig-killing took place in an outhouse in winter, "preferably when it was frosty. Bacon would cure and keep better than if you did t'killing in warm weather. My dad used to kill 'em sometimes. Or we'd get Bob Parker from Collyholme. My Uncle Jack used to kill pigs."

A luckless animal was "stuck wi' t'knife and bled. The blood was kept for black puddings. You kept stirring it and you put a handful of salt in to stop it from crudding [clotting]. Black puddings were made using groats [which was "on t'stamp of barley, and boiled first"], fat and seasoning—salt, pepper, thyme, even boiled onion, cut fine. The mixture was got to the consistency of thick cream and then you could pour it into the skins, using a big funnel."

The skins were t'puddings [intestines], turned inside out and scraped. It was generally thought of as "a mucky job". The puddings were boiled. If you did not put it in skins because there was no spare time; then it was poured into dishes "and slipped into th'oven to be cooked. For t'sausage job, a big mincing machine was available. You also needed a lot more skins. Sometimes you didn't even put sausage in skins. At Christmas, sausage meat by itself was eaten with turkey or goose."

Hanging from hooks attached to beams in the kitchen was the pigmeat—hams, shoulders and bacon, either in flick [flitch] or rolled. "It were said that when a pig was killed, only one thing was wasted and that was t'squeal." The rolls were tied with string using a special knot. The pork was generally hung "away from t'fireplace".

A woman reared at Dalehead remembers when "dad used to kill his own pigs, salting and rolling the meat. I have known the ham go off. You only needed to get a bluebottle in it and it would breed like mad if you didn't cut it away. Mother used to make brawn. Anyone would tell you about how good her brawn was."

A good goose laid its eggs in February and took a month to incubate them. George Robinson remembers when outdoor nesting sites were provided. The actual nest was made under tin sheeting which deflected the worst of the wind and rain. "T'owd gander could be vicious. Goose would leave the nest after covering it up with a bit of straw and she'd have a drink and a bit of a stroll. Then, if gander wasn't just about, we'd creep in to where t'nest was and have a look at those eggs. One time, when t'gander came, there I was! As soon as I came out, he clobbered me with his wings. He made me sit up . . ." A gander might even kill a lamb if it strayed too near.

The spare geese were killed one evening just before Christmas. Nothing much was wasted. The wings were dried and sterilised to be used as a substitute for a handbrush in the house. There was nothing quite so efficient as a goose-wing for catching cobwebs behind large pieces of furniture.

Plucking a goose was an arduous task. And it was such a "mucky business" it was generally carried out in an outbuilding. "A goose was to go over twice. When you'd pulled t'feathers off you had to 'dawn' em [remove the down]. You generally dawned 'em into a dolly tub. The softer feathers were sterilised and used for filling pillows or eiderdowns.

Goose grease, which was "smelly stuff", was said to be good for colds. "Mother would rub your chest with it. If it got rancid, it was used as dubbin for boots.

A farmer's wife kept the domestic fire burning continuously, even during the hottest weather in summer. It was the main source of hot water. Doris Wells, who was reared at Halsteads, recalls when peat was the main fuel. In an area with few fences and tracts of woodland, getting kindling for a fire was a problem.

"On a fine Saturday afternoon, mother would get a sack from the grainery and suggest that we children might go sticking, which we did, combing the thin woodland in the gills. A strong wind would prune the ash trees but because we were always going there, dead wood didn't accumulate."

As mentioned, every farm owed its existence to a handy supply of fresh water off the hill. This was stored in troughs or piped direct to the kitchen, where much of it was heated using a side boiler on an old-fashioned range which was black-leaded weekly. The weekly wash was carried out in a cast iron set-pot with a fireplace beneath it. The boiler was usually filled on Monday morning.

Doris Wells was familiar with the routine of drawing water in buckets from stone troughs at the front of the farmhouse. Water reached the troughs from the moor by way of a stone field drain. If the drain was blocked, a tell-tale wet mark appeared in the field and the farmer or his man dug down to clear it. Invariably, the hole was left unfilled so that "cows went and drunk there, then turned round and did what they had to do. Straight into the water. But we are still living to tell the tale."

When the big kettle was to be left overnight, it was always emptied and fresh water added for the morning brew-up. Water boiled twice gave a funny taste to tea and, when milk was added had a blueish tint.

What affected the tea might also cause annoyance on wash-day. Doris Wells's mother used the moorland water except when it went peat-brown. She would then save her snow-white sheets and pillow cases until the peatiness cleared and she had confidence in washing them without them becoming stained. "If they once got what mother called 'a bad colour' you couldn't get them white again."

In a dry summer, water in the galvanised tank became slimy. "It got as it was not fit to use."

Hired Help

People were content with what they had.

They're trying to farm out o' books now—and you can't.

A housekeeper who lived as one of the family might not get much money but she was well-fed and warm and had a good feather bed to sleep in.

Doris Wells.

WHEN Jonathan Slinger, of Cocklett End, married a Land Army girl shortly after the 1914-18 war, his wife performed the household duties which had hitherto been carried out by his unmarried sister.

A woman without offspring who had been widowed when still relatively young—say, about 45 years old—might find employment as a housekeeper, either becoming a member of a family or running the household for an elderly farmer who had been left alone. At a large farm, the staff might include both a housekeeper and a maid.

Jonathan Slinger's farm was too small for a hired man to be employed. In any case, by marrying a Land Army girl he ensured there would be someone young, strong and conversant with the farming routine. Cocklett End was "a good little farm" but labour was intensive. A "strapping lass" was vital for milking and butter-making. The rumble of an end-over-end churn was a familiar sound.

Doris Wells passed Cocklett End on her way between Halsteads (where she lived) and the village school.

When the Slingers' daughter was about eighteen months old, and it was haytime, the couple provided Doris with her tea on her homeward way and she would baby-sit for an hour or two, on two or three evenings a week, while they led some hay to the barn. "I might get a shilling at the end of the week."

When, for some eighteen months, Doris helped her grandmother (granddad was an invalid who had to be humped about) she was content with ten shillings a week. The South Lakeland lasses who were hired at Ulverston or who attended the hirings at Bentham received about the same amount of money when they were employed as domestic help.

Many a farmer's son found a wife—and the community some "new blood"—in a young woman from Barrow or Dalton-in-Furness. One such marriage took place between a Dalehead farmer and a Furness girl who had been a maid at Cappleside.

Tom Carr, of Halsteads, got his farm men "new off school". A servant lad had about £22 a year, being paid £11 at the end of each half year, but "he got kept and mother used to do his mending and washing. She just regarded him as one of the family. If a lad got that he wanted something new—such as working trousers—mother would get them for him and deduct the cost from his next payment, at Whitsuntide or November."

A Dalehead farmer in need of Irish labour for haytime made a point of visiting Bentham Fair. This involved getting to Clapham station, invariably on foot, and taking a train to Bentham. "There were some Taylors living at Greenfold. One of them had a hair-lip and talked a bit strange. He was the one who went to the hiring.

As they were walking back, and reached Bowland Knotts, Duckett Taylor would remark: "Well—we're back in England now'."

Bentham Fair was early in the summer; "we didn't want men for about a fortnight. What the Irishmen did in t'meantime I just do not know. If you went to Bentham, you got pick o' t'men but Bolton-by-Bowland hirings took place nearer haytime itself."

In wartime (1914-18), you got who you could. In 1917, an old chap from Durham was employed at Halsteads. Doris Wells says: "He'd come to t'Fair Hill when my grandfather was there."

An Irish helper was accommodated in the granary, where it was dry and warm. "There'd be an old bedstead and a flock mattress. And, of course, mother put sheets and blankets on just as she would have done if he'd been in the house." If the weather was fine, haytime took "just over a fortnight".

Horse Power

Willie Jackson was known to be hard on horses.

Th'osses were tired—and I wasn't feeling too fresh myself.

Robin Waddington.

WHEN Robin Waddington left school, he took up farm work. He was already accustomed to it, having been born and bred on a farm near Tosside. He also knew a bit about horses.

"I was with Willie Jackson, of Far Knotts. He was just a fair lad, I'll tell you, and he was a fair good horseman. In fact, he'd been a sergeant in t'first world war, training horses and then tekking 'em up to t'front line. It left him with a little bit of a limp. It didn't bother him."

Willie was a good boss, though he did have "a fair temper" and would get into "a reight tantrum" about something. "Then, all of a sudden, he'd be reight again. We were sat having our dinner one day. He finished, then mentioned a horse he'd been breaking it. Said Willie: 'Nah then, that hoss is fit to ride'. So we went out. He puts saddle on. We get into t'front meadow. He had t'bridle on it but he left th'halter on as well. He told me to stick to it while things got quietened down a bit.

"So he started trotting around t'meadow, me hold of th'halter. He kept going and going. I were getting fagged out. At t'finish, I said to him: 'Oh, tak thee owd 'oss'. And I threw th'halter up on to its neck. As soon as I did that, it started, rearing up at front end, then at back end. Willie finished up on 'is back in t'meadow. By gum, if he'd a caught me just then, I'd have bin for it. . ."

There came a time, in the early 1920s, when the ambitious Willie Jackson thought his farm near Tosside was not big enough for him. Robin was still working for him. "He took a reight big farm down Lune Valley. They called it Newton Hall. It was in between Whittington and Arkholme.

"It was better country than Tosside. One farmer in Lunesdale said to Robin: 'I hear thy stock can eat thi grass up at Far Knotts, but thou'll never eat it when thou comes down to Newton Hall'. Willie, who bragged a bit, said he'd show 'em when it came to eating grass. But it just about beat him."

Robin will never forget the time when Willie Jackson flit.

"It was t'spring end of t'year. There was a bit of snow on t'ground. They flit most of t'stuff in cattle wagons, but he said to me: 'Does ta think thou can tak 'oss and [two-wheeled] cart through to Newton Hall?' I said: 'That's a long way'. 'Ah', he said, but thou'll get it done in a day. Boss liked to get a move on; he didn't like dawdling."

The cart was fitted with "shelvings" which, as explained, were a light frame, used at haytime, which fitted across the cart, overlapping and giving it a bigger carrying capacity. The furniture—"dressers, chairs and bedroom stuff"—was loaded the previous day.

On the morning of departure, Willie considered that Robin might encounter roads that were "a bit slippy". He said he must "put t'sharps in". This meant that dummy studs were taken from the horses' shoes and replaced with pointed studs, which would let the animals grip the road surface of beaten earth.

Robin continued his tale: "I said to Willie—'If I'm going to take this lot to Lunesdale, I'll have something nice to sit on. An easy chair or something like that'. I put one on t'front shelving. He said: 'Thou's a crafty owd begger!'

"It had been snowing but I had a nice ride from Far Knotts, up Knott Hill and over to Four Lane Ends. And right through Dalehead. The road was rough in them days."

Robin had an ordinary Shire horse in the shafts—a horse which had been laid out all winter and was not in good shape. There was also a trace-horse tied to the back of the cart for use on a hill. "That trace-horse was a hackney which Willie used for delivering milk in a float. It would just help out. We didn't expect it to do a big lot. Yon hackney didn't fare so well in t'shafts of a heavy cart."

At Dale House, which stands beside the brow leading to Bowland Knotts, Robin had to review the situation. "When I set off there was a fair thickness of snow. When I got to Dalehead, sun had come out. It softened the snow, though this was bunging t'horses shoes up and they started sliding. At Dale House, Mr Hunt said: 'Come thee ways in. I had a drink o' tea and a chat.

He baited my hosses."

Robin said he must keep moving or he would never reach Lunesdale. Whereupon the farmer remarked: "I suppose thou will, but that horse thou has in t'shafts looks abaht jiggered. I've a big lazy old thing in t'stable doing nowt. I'll tak thee to t'top of t'Knotts."

Robin tied both of Willie Jackson's horses to the back of the cart and "this gurt strong thing took it reight to top of t'Knotts. I'd nearly done climbing then. It were all downhill to Keasden."

Early that morning, he had set off from Far Knotts at six o' clock and it was exactly twelve hours later when he arrived at Willie's new farm in Lunesdale. "I must have covered getting on for twenty miles."

When Robin worked for Jonathan Harrison, of Bottoms Farm, Dalehead, he had a lot to do with horses. The Harrisons eventually moved to a farm at Gisburn. "I worked for 'em a bit after they'd flit.

One day, when it were raining a bit and it were not fit for working out, Owd Mr Harrison says to me: 'Oh—thou mun clean that cart harness up this afternoon'. So I set to and cleaned it up. I polished t'leather and brasses. T'hames had got a bit rusty and so I sandpapered 'em and put a light oil on 'em. Oh, he come round and says: 'Thou hasn't done so bad'.

Then he picked these hames up and says: 'What's tha put oil on th'hames for?' 'Well', I says, 'It'll do 'em good. For one thing, it'll stop 'em rusting'. He looked down at me and says: 'Thou's a rust!' Aye—Jonathan Harrison was rather a droll 'un."

Margaret Jolly recalls: "Dad used to go for coal [from Raingill] over to Bentham with a horse and cart. He was a non-drinking man and would soon be back. His two brothers would get drunk on the way back and would not get back to their Dalehead farms on the same day."

The Vicarage, Dalehead.

Dalehead Church

Everyone wore a hard hat for a funeral. But you looked odd on a motor bike when you were wearing a hard hat.

Tom Cowking.

IT WAS comforting to know that Dalehead Church was there, even if you were not a regular attender at the services. On the major festivals or for christenings, weddings and funerals, the church was packed.

Tom Cowking remembers when a Daleheader was "bid" to a funeral. "It was just an extra acknowledgement, you might say. The bearers were specially bidden and, on some occasions, each bearer returned home with a new pair of black kid gloves, which he had worn while carrying the coffin."

One man had "any number of kid gloves" stacked up in a drawer but custom decreed that they were not used again. Leather, if not exposed to the air, goes mouldy. It happened to many pairs of Dalehead gloves.

The late Victorian period was a somewhat doleful time, presided over by a Queen in continuous mourning for her dead husband and with life so chancy there was a morbid fascination with death, as reflected by the black-edged funeral card with its few lines of verse and the name of the deceased.

Such cards were kept in tissue paper as though they would be needed on the Day of Resurrection. At one house, cards were kept tucked in notched wood which, framed in wood, was hung on a wall of the parlour as a reminder of the brevity of human life.

When a funeral service at Dalehead Church was over; when the mourners gathered in chattering groups, there was much speculation about the extent of the money left by the dear departed. A parson overheard two bearers talking. One said: "I wonder how much he's left." The parson interjected, saying: "I'm afraid he's left it all."

Funerals were grand occasions, with a big meal afterwards, "usually at the farmhouse but sometimes at the pub." It was a good meal, invariably featuring ham. The Daleheader was "buried wi' 'am."

Weddings were less flamboyant than they are today. A fading photograph shows a wedding group outside the Temperance Inn, the bride in Sunday best clothes rather than a white gown so familiar today. The celebratory meal took place before the "happy couple" resumed the daily round and common task. Honeymoons were uncommon.

The old Dalehead Church, dedicated to St James, stood beside the road from Four Lane Ends to Bowland Knotts and almost shouted to be noticed, having been built on a grand scale, with seating for 150, a high pulpit and a roof which rose steeply, as though determined to be seen from every farm in the parish.

The site for Church and Vicarage, plus an endowment of £50 per annum, had been the gift of William Wilkinson, of Hellifield, a prominent landowner at Dalehead. William Tillotson, of Shays Farm, Tosside, used to relate that when the church was consecrated by the first Bishop of Ripon, Charles Thomas Longley, DD (afterwards Archbishop of Canterbury) on October 27, 1852, the Bishop's representative should have presented the deeds to William Wilkinson but, confused by similar names, he handed them to King Wilkinson, of Slaidburn.

Nineteen years later, by an order in Council, some 9,000 acres of the ecclesiastical parish of Slaidburn was assigned to the new Dalehead parish, where the incumbent, who had the spiritual care of some 500 souls, was authorised to conduct baptisms, marriages and burials.

In 1915, the Rev Thomas William Castle became the incumbent of Dalehead. He had been serving a Derbyshire mining village and his parishioners gave him a horse and trap as a parting gift. Dalehead farmers supplemented the Vicar's stock of hay for the horse. Mr Castle was unusual as a parson, having served for 12 years as a missionary among the Blackfoot Indians of Western Canada.

Anyone who knows the upper Hodder valley, and who passes the newer church, originally a mortuary chapel, in its hallowed plot of ground, recalls the events of 1925—the transference of the remains of those interred in the old churchyard to the new burial ground, a tract of land consecrated on November 12, 1926, by Arthur, first Bishop of Bradford.

John Heap, interviewed by Graham Johnston for the *Lancashire Evening Post* in 1976, spoke of having helped to exhume 150 bodies buried up to 73 years earlier. "The gruesome ordeal of exhumation—the operation lasted for three weeks—still sends a shiver down his spine. In the sinister shadow of flare lights they removed tombstones and crumbling coffins behind hastily erected hessian screens. . . After the first night an official sent along by the local medical officer was so sickened that he went home saying he would rather lose his job than carry on."

Vic Robinson was still at Dale Head School when the workmen started moving graves from the Churchyard. "There was great amazement when they unearthed a wooden arm. The story goes that, years before, a farmer from Black House had been showing someone his stallion when it took his arm clean off and he had to wear that wooden one." Vic confirms that the graves were moved by night.

Eleanor Sedgwick, who was teaching at Dalehead School from

1925 until 1927, recalls the nocturnal activity. "I can remember staying at Tosside. I was going down the road on my bicycle and was approaching the school when I met this gang of men. I rang my bicycle bell but they seemed to be looking down. They took no notice of me, so I had to jump off to pass them. The time was perhaps a quarter to four; they would be on their way to work in the churchyard, which took place at night. During the day, canvas was set round where they had been. We never saw anything."

PUBLIC NOTICES.

FYLDE WATER BOARD.

NOTICE IS HEREBY GIVEN that under the provisions of Section 44 of the Fylde Water Board Act 1912 the Board propose to remove all remains of deceased persons interred in the Burial Ground of St. James' (otherwise the Parish Church of Dalehead) in the West Riding of the County of York.

Within two months after the first publication hereof any person who is an heir executor administrator or relative of any such deceased person may give notice to me in writing of his intention to undertake the removal of such remains for re-interment in any consecrated Burial Ground or Cemetery. Such removal may be without faculty but subject to any regulations made by the Bishop of Bradford.

If any person fail to satisfy the Board that he is such heir executor administrator or relative, the question shall be determined by the Registrar of the Consistory Court of the Diocese of Bradford.

The expense of such removal and re-interment (not exceeding £15 for remains from any one grave) shall be defrayed by the Board and apportioned if necessary according to the number of remains.

If within two months no such notice be given or after giving such notice the persons fail to comply with the above section and any regulations of the Bishop, the Board may remove and re-inter such remains in such consecrated Burial Ground or Cemetery as they think suitable subject to the consent of the Bishop.

All monuments and tombstones shall at the expense of the Board be removed and re-erected at the place of re-interment or at such place within the Parish as the Bishop may direct on the application (if any) of such heir executor administrator or relative as aforesaid or of the Board.

Dated this 13th day of August, 1925.

JOHN HALL,
Clerk and Solicitor.

Sefton-street, Blackpool.

Violet Cowgill, whose mother was one of the Robinson daughters from Stephen Park, recalls special Church treats, such as the Christmas tea and party, the annual sports in the Vicarage paddock and lawns, and the annual trip to Blackpool.

She and her family lived over three miles from the Church but she went to the services "wet or fine". Mrs Cowgill recalls a stormy morning in 1934 when she set off early and was well and truly soaked. "I remember running the last few hundred yards and up that tree-lined path to the Church porch and into Church—where there was not a soul.

"The building was so big and I felt so lonely. I went back to the porch and peeped out, through the pouring rain. Into view, through the little swing gate, came the Rev Cyril Slater. He went through the whole service for me, though we did not have any hymns. The organist—my cousin, Drina Robinson—had not managed to attend. At Christmastide, 1934, the Vicar gave Violet a book, noting on the flyleaf the service at which only two people were present.

Mr Slater had a Jowett car and occasionally gave lifts. Violet and Drina would sit in what was called the "dickie boot", with no protection from the elements, travelling in rain or sun. "At least we were not walking." When a farmhouse service was organised at Lamb Hill, the weather was foggy, particularly so when hometime arrived. "Mr Slater had the two of us walk all the way down to Slaidburn in front of his car, ensuring that he stayed on the road!"

As the reservoir work proceeded, it was announced that the Church, Vicarage and School would be demolished. In 1933, the organ had been installed in Trinity Methodist Church at Skipton. At the thanksgiving service, one of the items played was "Twilight" by Meale.

During 1934, the western part of Dalehead parish was re-united with Slaidburn and what remained, including the Burial Ground, came into the parish of Tosside. In May, 1936, when the last service at Dalehead was announced, the *Advertiser and Times* reported that it would be conducted by the Mr Slater, who had now accepted the living of Cundall with Norton-le-Clay, in the Diocese of Ripon. He was consequently the last clergyman to hold the living of Dalehead when it was a parish in its own account.

In accordance with the findings of a Commission appointed by the Bishop of Bradford, which heard evidence at Dalehead in May, 1932, the ecclesiastical parish ceased to exist on the termination of the incumbency of the vicar then in charge.

This decision was reached because of the small attendances at the services, "the decline having been caused by the removal of many families as a result of the Fylde Water Board constructing its new reservoir in the neighbourhood." Mr Slater was not able to reconcile himself to the Commission's views. For weeks, he sustained a lively correspondence in the Clitheroe newspaper. John Hall, a solicitor representing the Fylde Water Board, was somewhat scathing of the vicar's knowledge until he [the vicar] let it be known he was also a barrister. Hall apologised in print—and never wrote to the newspaper again.

It was Cyril Slater's assertion that the stipend of the Vicar was provided for and the people still remaining here were able to raise the amount required for church expenses. The neighbouring parish churches could not be as convenient of access, for some of the remaining residents had to travel more than two miles to Dalehead Church.

The Vicar added, sadly: "I do not suppose that there are now a hundred people left in Dalehead parish. The average attendance at church for both morning and evening services has been nine. There were more communicants on Easter Day this year than on any day since I came here. On that occasion we had seventeen." Dalehead had two splendid churchwardens in John Peel of

Brookhouse Green and Stephen Robinson of Stephen Park.

The newspaper understood that the parish church and the vicarage had been purchased by the Fylde Water Board, who would shortly demolish them. "From the material obtained from the removal of the church, a small chapel is to be built in the new cemetery provided further up the valley."

The parish itself was to be divided, the larger portion being transferred to Slaidburn and the smaller to Tosside. "The dividing line runs down the Clapham road from Bolland Knotts, along the new road by the reservoir and thence by what is known as Old House lane to the cross roads and on to Champion. The land north and east of this line will become part of Tosside..."

Of the income, £200 was to be used for clerical or lay assistance in Slaidburn's enlarged parish and £60 would be added to the stipend of the Rector. The remaining portion of the £303 would augment the stipend of the Vicar of Tosside.

A newspaperman added: "The demolition of church and vicarage will cause more than a pang of regret among the many families who regard Dalehead as home and among the families of the seven vicars who have served the parish during the eighty-four years the church has stood."

The last service took place on May 24, 1936. Violet Cowgill recalls that the church was "packed to the door", despite heavy rain during the afternoon and evening. Old Mrs Slinger, of Forest Becks, had walked the eight miles to attend the morning service. The evening service was preceded by a christening ceremony, the infant being Marion Walmsley, of Black House, whose great grandparents had been the first couple to be married at Dalehead when the church was opened eighty-four years before.

Fylde Water Board covered the cost of building the present Dalehead Church, using stone from the old building. The present Church was consecrated by the assistant Bishop of Bradford on

July 30, 1938. The east window consists of stained glass in three panels, placed there to the memory of Isabella, wife of William King Wilkinson, who died on May 22, 1900.

Today, a small regular congregation meets for a service at 2 p.m. on the third Sunday in every month. The congregation swells to occupy all the available seating several times a year, such as the Harvest Festival and at Christmas.

The church is left open, despite the risk of theft and vandalism, and many people sign the visitors' book. A childless couple prayed for the gift of children; their prayers were answered and their children subsequently baptised at Dalehead.

In 1993, an appeal was launched to cover the cost of pointing, attending to the roof and guttering and other work, at an estimated cost of about £9,000.

The Travellers' Rest.

Tales Out of School

When I went to Dalehead School, there'd be about seventy-two children on the register. Usually there were just over thirty ordinary Daleheaders. So there were quite a few extra children when the reservoir was being built.

George Thompson.

About half the children are called Robinson and are distinguished from each other by the place where they live.

E Buck (1913).

DALEHEAD SCHOOL was a substantial structure of stone and slate. A carved stone high on one end of the building had the inscription: "The fear of the Lord is the beginning of knowledge." Standing near the school was the parish hearse house. The hearse was a sombre-looking conveyance, with large carved black urns, not unlike pinnacles, at each corner.

The interior of Dalehead School was divided into two rooms—one big, with a teacher and class at each end, the other room being used for storage purposes. Access to the building was through one of two porches. The playground was rough. Children frequently ran to the teachers with bleeding knees, wanting medical attention.

Heating was provided by a central stove. "It was very cold first thing in the morning because it had not been lit for very long. When the first playtime came, the children would gather around for a warm."

Jim Leeming had a remarkable school record—six years' full

attendance. "My folk were the caretakers," he explained. Jim had to light the school stove and put out a dish of water to maintain a degree of humidity. Wet days saw the children's clogs placed near the fire. The fireguard was used for drying out wet garments.

When Eleanor Haigh, a native of Cotehill near Carlisle, took up a job at Dalehead School in 1925, it was her first teaching appointment. She already knew the dale country, being reared in Dent and mid-Airedale. She had not passed the medical examination but Mr Appleby, who was the headmaster at Kildwick, advised her that if she would like to become a teacher, she should apply "for an out-of-the-way post that nobody wants." Then a local doctor might be consulted.

"I got the West Riding vacancy list and chose two places which were quite a distance from a railway station. And there were no buses. Dalehead stood nine miles from Long Preston. Garsdale was four miles from Hawes Junction."

She was granted an interview at Dalehead and set off by train to Long Preston, her parents recommending that she hire a taxi from Long Preston. None was available. She walked to Dalehead, in quite good weather.

"When I got to Tosside I could have had a horse and trap but I thought I could manage the next four miles." The first person she spoke to was the school caretaker. She directed me to the Vicarage, where the interview was to take place.

The Rev Morris, a tall, dark Lancashireman, had spiritual charge of Dalehead. Did she remember his first name? "No. You didn't use first names as much in those days." Also present at the interview was the schoolmaster. "When the interview was over, I got a good meal, with ham carved by the vicar. Then they rang up for a taxi. So I was all right."

The vicar and schoolmaster accompanied her in the taxi to Long Preston. "I think it was a night out for them." As the car passed a gate, she was aware she had got the job when the vicar said: "Oh, you'll be staying at a farm down that lane."

Having been notified she had got the job, she passed the 'medical' through a doctor in Cross Hills. Then, on a wild March day, with heavy showers of hail, she boarded a draughty taxi at Long Preston station for her return to Dalehead.

"I wasn't sure where my lodgings were, but eventually she followed a rough cart track to inquire, returning to tell him they had the right place [a farm near Raingill]. The taximan then drove me down with my luggage."

The farmer and his wife, Mr and Mrs Jack Peel, were friendly but thrifty. They also went to bed early. "I got into trouble one night for coming in late. The farmer was sitting up waiting for me. He looked angry and said: 'I've got to get up in a morning'."

Mrs Peel had a backstone on which she had once made oatcake. She would take a basketful in the direction of Clitheroe and sell it. And when I was there she had just got a knitting machine. She knit jerseys for her three children and then started knitting silk stockings. I think that I bought the first pair she made.

They had one or two faults and they were a bit thicker than the ones we have today."

The accommodation was adequate, the food plain, as it was elsewhere in the valley. For the main meal, there would be "potatoes and some kind of meat. I remember having cow's heart, lean meat that was very dry. Suet or milk puddings generally formed the "sweet".

The new teacher had to attend to her charges within earshot of the schoolmaster. She soon recognised his worthiness as a teacher. "He had passed all his exams without going to college. And he really could give a very interesting lesson."

At Dalehead, "we stuck to the Three Rs, and then had a bit of geography, a bit of history, nature study, physical training and singing. I had to take singing when the headmaster was out supervising physical training. And vice versa."

The children were mainly from the farms. "They were very nice children. For a short time I had two boys who walked three and a-half miles to school from Fair Hill. [Eleanor's future father-in-law had started farming at Fair Hill many years before]. The elder boy did not start school until the other was old enough and so one was five and the other six and a-half years old at the time their names went on the register.

"But they were not there long. I remember them arguing with each other one day in school about where they were going to go. One said Australia and I think the other said Canada. So which they did go to eventually, I don't know.

"And then for a time we had the children from Hollins navvy village and various lodgings." Some children were not as fastidious as the farm children. A number did not arrive at school on time—despite the urgent clanging of the school bell at 8-50 a.m. to give warning. "If any of the missing children were living close at hand, the headmaster would send someone to ask about them. Were they still in bed?" In very wet weather, some of the children did not attend school, having to walk two or three miles each way.

One winter weekend, when Eleanor had been home, she left the train at Long Preston station on her return journey. Collecting her bicycle, she set off hopefully for Dalehead. "I was all right for the first two miles. Then, as I got higher, I found the snow was deeper.

"By the time I got to Tosside, I had to carry the bicycle. I walked into Dalehead School almost three hours late and was greeted with 'It will be half a day's pay off'. I don't think it was." [She was paid £96 a year "and later on, when I was head of a small country school, I started at £172."]

Eleanor Haigh married Septimus Sedgwick, and "he used to tell me all sorts of tales about Dalehead. There was a schoolmaster called Mr Barron. Two of the Hanson boys of Bridge House were always playing tricks on him. Mr Barron, went there for his milk and the two boys would be sitting, as good as gold, on each side of the fireplace.

"As soon as he went out at the front door, with his jug of milk they went out at the back and, keeping out of sight, held some string across the road. The headmaster tumbled over the string and spilt his milk. He also probably broke the jug. The luckless man had to go back for more. When he reached the farm, the two lads would be sitting by the fire. No one suspected them."

Mr Barron had an apple tree in the schoolhouse garden. Overnight, six nice apples disappeared. He had a swill tub in which scraps of food were thrown to be fed to the pigs. The farmers' sons propped the tub against the headmaster's back door and, the next time he opened it, a mass of smelly food went all over his kitchen floor.

"The worst trick of all was when they got his white dog and put it in a tar barrel. The schoolmaster told the police about this and, of course, the Sedgwicks—being a big family—were blamed. The Sedgwick lads, watching through a slit in the barn, saw the arrival of the police.

"Who dropped the dog into the tar was kept a perfect secret. My husband, after we lived at Hanlith, in the 1940s, went to the auction and found out for the first time who'd done that to the dog. It was not the Sedgwicks at all but a 'nice quiet chap' who was also one of the school managers. You wouldn't have thought he could do such a trick." Incidentally, Mr Barron became head of Clapham School.

"Daddy" Price—whose real name was William—was one of the headmasters who had a no-nonsense approach to education in the days when Vic Robinson went to school. Vic also remembers being taught by Miss Haigh.

He began in 1921, when he was seven years old, and he and his brother Ted were expected to deliver milk, in cans, on their way to school. "We'd never a lazy moment. . .we'd a lot to do." Vic's customers were the schoolmaster, parson, resident engineer (for the Fylde Water Board was now firmly in control) and the Traveller's Rest.

"We wore clogs. If it came a snow, clogs used to 'ball up' underneath till it was not easy to walk. Sometimes I'd go flat on my back, holding cans of milk, and I'd spill one lot. I'd put the others behind a wall and go back home for some more milk. Then I'd turn up at school late. Daddy Price would say: 'And where have you been, Robinson?' 'Please, sir, I spilt the milk and had to go back home.' I'd have to do fifty lines—'I must not be late'."

Mr Deadman, a much revered schoolmaster, took his scholars to the waterworks scheme, where the engineers explained the processes. Mr Cottam, the resident engineer, was fond of recalling that the scholars had to write essays about what they had seen. He then invited Mr Cottam to the school, where he read out the best essays and gave a fully description of the topics raised.

"I don't know how the education given at Dalehead compares with that given in the newer schools," the engineer was to recall, "but I doubt if children of the same age are as good at arithmetic and writing as those village children were."

Mr Killick, the last schoolmaster to serve Dalehead, once spoke to photographer Buck about the loneliness of the place. He said that anyone who had been there for three years deserved to be moved to another place, though he had been much attached to the people.

Buck's photographs of Dalehead classes indicate that in 1914, seventeen girls and seventeen boys were attending school. Ten years later, "there was quite a good class. I makes you wonder where all the children came from."

George Robinson recalls when a child attending school from one of the remoter farms took some food for mid-day. "It wasn't much—just a few sandwiches. We ate them when we were running about and playing. We never had anything to drink. It was only the cold water tap in t'porch. We had a dinner when we got back home."

Margaret Jolly recalls: "When I went to school, with the children from Black House, we sometimes got a lift on Mr Cottam's railcar."

At Tosside School, a much-remembered headmaster was Mr Fox. "What his first name was I don't know, to tell you the truth. We always used to call him Old Fox," says Robin Waddington. He departed in mysterious circumstances. Young Robin Waddington, who lived at Middle Knotts, was walking to school early one morning, with his good pal Harold Metcalfe, when a horse and trap was seen coming down from Tosside.

"Mr Lawson, who had t'Temperance Hotel in them days, was driving that trap. Sitting with him was Old Fox and—a policeman. And Old Fox looked as stern as owt. They were taking him down to t'Courthouse at Bolton-by-Bowland. He got three years in prison. We kids never got to know anything about it."

Robin, born in 1907, had a walk of two miles to school. "We walked to Tossit School, hail, rain, snow or sunshine. Now they can't walk two strides afore they'll have to be getting on a bus."

The death of Mrs Collinge, the schoolmistress, affected the children deeply. They wept openly as the coffin was being carried into church for the funeral. Yet mention of her name also brings a smile to Robin's face. "We didn't half catch it once. She'd sent us out gardening. When she went round a bit after, all t'gooseberries had gone. That upset her."

Those who taught at Tosside School had to be prepared for rebellion. "During one lesson, Ernie Hodgson—a reight fiery lad—had got some sums wrong and he wouldn't try to put 'em right and teacher got t'stick [cane] out. Ernie said: 'If thou strikes me, I'll go home'. Teacher came for him, but Ernie was out and away. We didn't see him no more."

Edmundson Buck

THE PHOTOGRAPHIC career of Edmundson Buck, who left us a comprehensive record of the buildings of Dalehead, extended from 1890 until 1930. Buck was born at Brierfield in 1860 and his wife, Susannah, hailed from Colne. They had two sons—Harrison (born 1881) and David (born at Foulridge, 1883).

The 1891 census shows the Bucks to be living at 25 Peel Street. He was a cooper, employed at the Waterloo Brewery, but photography became a hobby and after the closure of the Brewery in about 1904 it was his full-time job.

Clitheroe was already well-served by photographers, no less than six being noted by *Slater's Directory of Lancashire* (1895). These were Robert T Coates, J Forrest and Son, George Harvey, Albert Parker and Benjamin Satterthwaite.

Buck was listed as a cooper in *Barrett's Directory of Blackburn and District* (1906) and had become a photographer, operating from 49 Waddington Road, Blackburn, in the 1906 issue of the same directory. In 1909, Buck, Edward [sic] was still in business.

In the Clitheroe days, Buck was a keen Churchman, an enthusiastic naturalist and a local historian who used the pen and plate camera for his records. His illustrated articles on the Ribble and Hodder valleys popularised that area throughout East Lancashire.

John Barry, himself a photographer, whose work appears in the *Clitheroe Advertiser,* has over 750 photographic studies by Buck and has painstakingly researched his public life. A note in the *Clitheroe Advertiser and Times* for March 21, 1890 mentions Buck, who at that time "entertained members of the Parish Church Mutual Improvement Society with a talk entitled An Evening with the Camera." John Barry has Buck's notes for a lecture on Bowland as The Switzerland of England. This event was in 1934, when Buck was 74 years old.

Buck inscribed each plate with "E Buck, Clitheroe". In view of this, it was appropriate (if uncomplimentary) to find this short verse:

> If ever you chance to see
> A man's name written on glass—
> Be sure he owns a diamond
> And his father owns an ass.

For thirty years, Buck maintained a picture postcard trade with the Robinsons of Stocks Fold. He never lost his excitement at visiting the upper Hodder valley, such as in about 1930, his experiences leading in due course to the appearance of an illustrated article in the *Clitheroe Advertiser.* This feature was subtitled "Pictures and Memories of a Vanished Village".

Buck and two companions walked to Dalehead. "We went to Slaidburn one day and stayed overnight, starting from there after an early breakfast." They were "fully equipped with sandwiches and cameras". Buck had not previously gone beyond Catlow.

Having arrived at the head of the dale, the three explorers spread out, looking for a spring of water. They arranged to meet up in an hour's time to compare notes. "None of us had found anything like a spring. The courses were all nearly dry, it being August. All the water was from drainings, swamp and moss beds."

The disappointed men had covered a hundred yards on the

return journey when they saw water trickling down a slope at the roadside. "Tracing this, we found it coming under the road through a drain pipe. We followed it up the channel till we came to a big stone and there we found a beautiful spring of crystal clear water. So delighted were we that my friend dipped in his drinking cup and we quaffed the clear water to our satisfaction that we had found the true source of the beautiful river."

The spring lay on the Catlow side of the valley, "a long way past the farm—about 200 yards from the top, where one can see over to Bentham. A waft of wind either way would take the rainfall either into the Hodder or the Lune." They followed the stream down to the first bridge, "called Cross Roads", and then down again to the old sheep folds for washing purposes; then on again to Kenibus, the Keeper's Cottage.

The Keeper, sitting in the field corner, had been watching them through binoculars. "We expected a good scolding but nothing happened. Perhaps he thought he had better say nothing, as it was a case of three to one—rather big odds."

It was now late afternoon. While Buck photographed Colleyholme, his friends went on to the New Inn at Stocks Fold to ask Mrs Robinson [a former neighbour of Buck in Clitheroe] to make them all a good tea. On one of the photographer's early visits, she had shown him a window pane on which the following words were scratched:

Bowland, Bowland, thy roads are rough,
And people's manner worse.
To live in such a country,
I should think it a great curse.

On another pane of the same window was the following:

The man who wrote on the other pane
Has never been here before;

I feel quite sure that he's insane
And ought to live on a moor (no more).

The second verse had been added by Dr J J Smithies, for many years the doctor of the Union. He often visited Dalehead, stopping at the inn, and had resented the comments which had been scratched on the window pane.

In his newspaper article, Buck related that after Mrs Robinson's occupation, the house was sold to John Swale, the village wheelwright, who had it modernised and converted into The Traveller's Rest and the Post Office, though without a licence for the sale of intoxicants.

Edmundson Buck died in 1941. The writer of his obituary recalled that "since coming to Clitheroe, Mr Buck had allied himself with the Parish Church and until attaining his eightieth birthday he rang the tenor bell." He was a zealot in the cause of the Sunday School, was associated with the Adult School movement and with the work of the Co-operative Education Committee."

At the age of 74, he had still been lecturing on his beloved Dalehead.

Ellen Cowking's Poems

Off to the fell ye men and dogs,
To gather the ewes, wethers and hogs.
Young lambs frisking, and jumping about
The shepherds they clap their hands and shout.

It's hardly great verse, but the poetry of Ellen Cowking, penned early this century, is at least lively and entertaining. Ellen was "a real poet", turning all her lines. Like many another rural poet of her day, she was topical and sentimental. Ellen had a strong pride in her farming background; she was devoted to the church and fiercely patriotic.

Our poet was born in 1863 and married William Cowking at St James's, Dalehead, on January 18, 1892. William, the hind at Lamb Hill, was nicknamed Curl. His wife was "good with her hands", being an outstanding cook and so accomplished at needlework that she had the confidence to send some of her work off as a gift to Royalty.

In other ways, she was a strange woman. She often locked up the pantry door and disappeared "up the hill" to write her verse, remaining away from home for hours on end.

Ellen bore Will five children, the first-born being christened William after his father. William and his brother Emmanuel Stephen (born 1896) were known at Dalehead for their practical jokes. Visiting Merrybent, they covered the kitchen chimney. When the room filled with smoke, Farmer Johnson immediately knew what was amiss and who was to blame. (In the reservoir-building days, Emmanuel was well-known as the pianist at the cinema established at Hollins, the navvy's village).

The third child of Will and Ellen was named after mother, being also given the name Mary, though everyone called her Nellie. (Her "life history", printed in *The Farmers' Weekly,* was dealt with in the section for Lamb Hill). A fourth child, Jennie, who was well educated, became a stylish letter-writer and something of an eccentric, especially with regard to the teaching of children.

Jennie insisted that when a child was learning to read, he or she "must be listened to as well as simply read to." Her confidence and ability in expressing herself once impressed the judge in a court case when she was representing herself. Jennie married Richard Carr and moved to Tinklers.

We return to Ellen, the poetess. She had the Victorian fascination with death and the life to come, and this was expressed in her verse. For example, Grace Hanson, a little servant girl, was "gathered" by the heavenly reapers and is now "in the bright land over there."

Ellen's own faith was soon to be tested by the loss of her ten-year-old son, Thomas, from injuries sustained when he fell in the barn at Lamb Hill. A poem about Thomas, written by Ellen, was called "Mother's Little Boy". As for everyday incidents and events in the farming calendar, Ellen had a sharp eye, a retentive mind, and a quiet sense of humour.

Now, through Ellen's poems, let us imagine ourselves at Dalehead early this century. The horse is master of the dusty road. The Hodder ripples between banks edged by fine trees. The air is flavoured by peat smoke from farmhouses on the green floor of the dale and also along the clayey upper slopes. There is not a Water Board official in sight!

One of Ellen's most ambitious poems concerns the sheep-clipping at Lamb Hill. Friends and neighbours come together to do the work in a single day and deal with the sheep at another big Dalehead farm on another day. If, because of poor weather, one farm's stock cannot be clipped at the appointed time, the farm must go "to the back of the queue".

Ellen's poem about Lamb Hill Clipping, written in November 1903, runs to thirty verses and captures the large scale of the operation, the noises and the bustle of the event, beginning with the rounding up of the ewes and their bemused lambs, a task for the morning of the previous day:

> The dogs are running and yelping too,
> To the old sheep it is nothing new.
> The lambs are capped [surprised], as well they may,
> Not understanding the clipping day.

When the sheep are in the fold:

> The dogs lie down or run about,
> Very pleased they are no doubt,
> The men drink gills of ale and gin,
> Again to work they now begin.

Soon it is time for lunch, which is provided in a basket, with a bottle of ale and can of tea to slake the thirst. Then the pre-clipping routine continues. Pens and stocks [wooden seats, adequate for man and sheep] must be arranged. Some of the clippers are inclined to arrive early on the following day:

> The men land up in two's and three's,
> They out with their shears, turn up their sleeves,
> In overalls blue and overalls white
> They clip away from morn to night.
>
> Some bring their daughters, some their wives,
> They cook, wash dishes and polish the knives,
> When all have got seated with sheep on the stocks,
> Some men take the fleeces, some pick up the locks [of wool].

Jobs are various. Boys catch unclipped sheep and take them to the clippers, collecting a shorn ewe, which must now be marked. The farmer and his wife ensure that no one is hungry or thirsty. Women move around with baskets and pots. On offer are sandwiches, custards and tarts.

> This meal now over, click again go the shears,
> Sometimes with a noise that nigh deafens your ears;
> But all passes off in the old style and old way,
> And soon is completed one more clipping day.

When the helpers sit down for dinner, the principal item on the menu is sirloin, "the old English joint". The men dine first, and then the women have a share, for "it would be a poor clipping if ladies weren't there."

> They now have got seated in one of the rooms
> Bye and bye you will hear some very good tunes.
> And presently the master thanks all his neighbours
> For their united kindness and united labours.
>
> He brings bowl of whisky and this is passed round;
> Very soon after, you will hear a good sound.
> When some old friend has had a good sup
> He'll sing a good song that livens all up.

The chief entertainer "shakes his old rig", an indication he means "to give them a jig". First he needs "a wee drop of gin and a glass of good beer". Now that the lasses have finished their tasks, dancing begins. Some dancers are off to the loft; "others wait to be asked." The instruments are fiddle and concertina. Refreshments—tea, coffee, cake—are passed round. Some of the dancers sip port wine.

> Before the day breaks, some make their way home,
> But most of the young ones wait 'till the dawn.
> The skylarks may tell us, as they soar near the sky,
> They have been disturbed as the lovers pass by.

It has been an exhausting time for clippers and for Ellen Cowking, the poetess:

> They are all a bit sleepy,
> And my pen's sleepy too.
> To the clipping and clippers
> I will now say Adieu.

Also in 1904, Ellen deals with the busking activity of the Slaidburn Band (master, Mr Dud) as they stride from farm to farm at Dalehead. She mentions people and places.

The Slaidburn Band did take their way,
On this bright December day.
A band of young men, brave and smart,
For Hammerton Hall they made a start.

The bandsmen pause to play Christmas music at Raingill, Brookhouse Green, Black House and Bridge House, Cocklett House and Eggbury.

To the Mister and Misses Cowkings
Of Grange they next do come;
The old couple there has passed away,
But they play tunes for the young.

To the New Inn and Post Office,
'Tis known best by Stocks Fold,
They play hymns ancient and modern,
Songs, dances, new and old.

From here there have been changes,
'Twas here Charlie won his bride,
But now she's gone to live with him
At New Close to reside.

The band visit the School House (where they beguile Mr Agar) and Swinshaw (to greet a newly-married couple) and on to the Vicarage (much hand-shaking with the vicar).

He delights to see the Slaidburn Band
Come round from year to year;
But he hopes to see them all again,
When the summer draweth near.

Much later, the bandsmen are at Higher Croft House, Higher Birch House, Hasgill, New House and Collyholme. Then:

The Band to Kenibus next must come,
The evening now is drawing on.

The sun has set behind the hills,
Sun, moon and stars, God's law fulfil.

So to Lamb Hill, where the bandsmen linger for a while before playing "Auld Lang Syne" and departing for home.

In February, Ellen takes up her pen to praise Nurse Price, "the nurse, you know, who is so nice." She is also very clever, "forget her, could we? Oh no, never." This conscientious District Nurse is a smoother of pillows and raiser of the sinking heart.

Ponder on "Johny The Post", a poem which has such a slow start he is first mentioned in verse eight and begins his postal work in verse eleven:

He manfully does
His duty each day.
Delivers and receives,
Letters by the way.

In October, 1904, Dalehead in general and the Cowkings in particular are stunned by the death of Thomas Cowking, of Lamb Hill, aged ten years. Reference has already been made to her poem, "Mother's Little Boy", giving us an insight into the Victorian attitude towards death.

The poem mentions "the angel of death" and the "valley of death", "the better land" and "the golden shore". At the funeral service:

Solemnly Mr Johnson prays,
Exhorts them all and then he says—
Fear ye the Lord, take heed in time,
Thou can'st not call tomorrow thine.

Mr Garnett speaks and looks above,
And points us to the heavenly dove,
As on the coffin the sun doth shine,
May Christ shine in your hearts and mine.

Ellen now writes with wry humour about the "King of the mountains, old boy of the fells". There was a time when he was young and bold. He enjoyed his jaunts to the hills. But now old age is creeping on. His footsteps are feeble, his hair turning grey. . .

> But still the boy, good company can keep,
> With a talk of the wool trade, the grouse or the sheep.
> He still has a liking for a wee drop of gin,
> But whoever heard tell of a teetotal King?

How a young man's "quinsy" is dealt with by the doctor is the subject of another poem, from which are culled these lines relating to the do's and dont's of this painful swelling of the throat. A fire is kindled in the sufferer's bedroom; he is not allowed out of bed, even as far as the door.

The doctor must be summoned as soon as possible. While waiting his arrival, make the sufferer comfortable:

> Put a bottle to his feet
> And let it be right hot;
> And tuck him round with blankets
> Like a baby in its cot.

The doctor peeps down the sufferer's throat and finds it red.

> . . . Oh yes, it's quinsy, sure and good,
> Bring water, boiling, in a gallon jug."
>
> And steam him well in the mouth and throat
> Or else he'll happen go and choke.
> Steam him well twelve times a day
> And give him gruel and currant taie [tea].

The doctor promises to send medicine, "some for to gargle and some to sup". The sufferer must be given a sup of elder wine. The quinsy bursts; now is the time for more gargling, some bitter beer and a pot of stout.

Feed him up, feed him well,
He'll soon be able to "look" the fell.

Ellen proclaims with another poem that "he who will not work should not eat":

Some men when their masters are in sight
Work like good un's with all their might,
But when their master is away
They are hardly worth a bob a day.
It is mid forenoon before ere a stroke
Is put at all unto their work.
With hands in pocket and pecker down
They ken their master's away at town.

When doing any kind of work, be particular:

Now Alice, when you wash the plates
Be sure to wipe them dry,
For if you don't, the plates and you
Will both be sure to cry.

Don't rush into marriage:

Charlie [Cowking] was a bachelor
Not much of him we know;
But all the lasses round about
Consider he is slow.
But never mind a bachelor,
In honour give him due—
He'd better bide a bachelor
Than marry, and then rue.

Grange Hall Farm.

The Dalehead Postman

JOHN RAWSTHORNE, of Slaidburn, who was known to Ellen and her family (as her poem about him testifies) carried the mail to Dalehead homes for four decades. He walked sixteen miles a day, six days a week, which means that he and his mailbag covered a total of almost 180,000 miles. John retired in August, 1929.

His round took in Lamb Hill, Catlow, Bowland Knotts and Dale House Bridge. Only once did he miss his round, and that was in extreme winter weather. After snow clogged the landscape, the postman set out only to stop beyond Hammerton Hall on finding the body of Mr Hartley, of Chapel House. This farmer, who was known to have heart trouble, had collapsed and died from exposure when returning from Slaidburn, where he had recorded his vote in an election.

Saturday came. A further heavy fall of snow gave the countryside a semi-arctic appearance. This was the day when Mr Hartley was to have been buried but drifts up to ten feet high blocked the road. The house was cut off.

John Rawsthorne had to wait until 3.15pm for the mail which should have reached him from Clitheroe in the early morning. Head Office told him not to attempt the round that day; he managed to deliver the mail, despite many difficulties, on Sunday. (When, finally, it was possible for Mr Hartley's body to be interred, a path through the snow had to be cut almost all the way from Dale Head to Gisburn).

When he began his career, the mail was light; it increased greatly with official mail during the reservoir-building period. In his young days, John Rawsthorne set off on foot for pleasure as well as business. "Many is the time I have walked to Clitheroe Fair after having done my sixteen mile round and then walked back home to Slaidburn in the early hours. We returned in parties and merry times we had, though we often wished we could lie down and sleep at the roadside. It was a good job that next day was Sunday, when we could stay in bed."

In his later years on the Dalehead round, the valley was being transformed and, with the closing down of many of the farms, land was untended and the grass grew unhindered, draggling his feet.

John Rawsthorne, the postman, retired when he reached his sixtieth birthday.

Stocks Fold.

A Watery Grave

Out in the quiet hills above Slaidburn, standing on a platform perched on the edge of a mighty lake, Prince George pressed an electric button and released the captured waters of the moors into the service of mankind.

Advertiser and Times, July 8, 1932.

After many years of strenuous and unremitting labour, success has crowned our efforts and we can rest on our laurels.

Councillor G B Robertson, at the opening.

. . . thus has been laid the bogey of a water famine in the Fylde.

The Manchester Guardian (July 6, 1932).

What wasn't drowned was abandoned . . .

Horace Cook.

A VISITOR to the shanty village of Hollins in 1925 stared with amazement at the site of the new dam and commented: "After two years of effort, a tremendous trench has been scarred right across the valley, from one hilltop to the other. It is seventy or eighty feet deep in parts and has gone down to the solid rock.

"This trench is for the big dam which will eventually hold back the water of the Hodder. Through the side of one of the hills, a huge tunnel is being driven. Centred round the trench is all kinds of evidence of activity—steam cranes, derricks, stone breakers, stagings, concrete mixing machines, excavators, rock drills, compressed air machines and such like appliances.

"The hillsides seem to be alive with little locomotives whose ceaseless puffing and whistling and scurrying with strings of little wagons prove what work is being done. Looking up the valley . . .

one sees a winding vista, with farms, houses, fields, a road and even a churchyard, all of which will be submerged when the great dam begins to hold back the water."

A cross-section of the embankment which the Fylde Water Board built to impound the upper Hodder resembles a sandwich cake. The engineers—more precisely, the Irish navvies and ex-miners recruited from Durham and Wales—went down to bedrock, of course, which they promptly smothered with a layer composed of 11,876 cubic yards of concrete.

There followed a layer composed of 69,842 cubic yards of puddled clay, the puddling being carried out by the tramping of human feet. A steel plate separated the clay from the clay and cement of the main part of the dam wall. On the reservoir side, the tunnel opening was sealed by a steel plate bulkhead, backed by concrete. The downstream side was finished in dressed stone, quarried from Jumbles, near the source of the Hodder.

The dam—1,173 feet long, 140 feet deep and with a mean width of 700 feet—was built to resist the pressure of 250,000 tons of water at whatever might prove to be its weakest section.

A visitor in 1928 was fascinated by the "puddle". He wrote: "We found that, as in most other things, there is an art in making puddle. It is trodden down into a thick and glutinous mass by men specially detailed for the task, with the result that a substance is obtained not unlike the mud which some of us knew so well on Salisbury Plain and in Flanders. It certainly has the same sticky properties..."

Harry Cottam, the resident engineer, was described by one visiting journalist as "a kindly ruler". George Thompson, of Slaidburn, recalls him as "a nice fellow, fairly tall and dark". Violet Cowgill, whose family knew the Cottams well, once heard him say about the initial work at the site of the dam: "We just dropped the whole bag of cement into the hole to start the job!"

"All the stuff—including the metals for the railway—came from the "dock" beside the main line at Long Preston. The first stage was by road, using enormous traction engines as motive power, hauling trailers bearing heavy rails. These monsters had wheels with steel spikes that ensured they would keep a grip on the road. "Well—they ground all up, you know."

George Robinson heard it said that ordinary farm carts with wooden, iron-rimmed wheels found the going heavy, the axles themselves scraping along the ground. "It was such a mess."

Robin Waddington and his school pals sat on a wall at Tosside and watched the engines surmounting the brow from Ribblesdale. "One was a traction engine and t'other was a little Fordson thing. Not as big. They had trailers at back on 'em.

"What a terrible state t'road got into. It got so bad they closed it down for a while till they'd mended it. There was a chap called Huddleston at Snape House and he about made his fortune on t'job. He had a quarry, got all t'stone out and was carting it for 'em."

Robin ruefully remembers when some lads spent too much time watching the Water Board traffic. "We got into hot water sometimes. We were theer when we should have been back at school."

The depot was at Tosside. "They started in half way between Chapel and Bond Beck bridge. They made a big yard so they could store stuff. Then they built a railway right across country. Us lads went down [from Tosside School] one dinnertime. There was a chap called Joe Parker. He had a spade. Joe said: 'Here—this is first sod o' t'Water Board'. He cut a sod out there and then. . ."

Work on the Stocks dam began in 1923, at which time the Water Board closed a temporary encampment at Greenfold quarry and developed the "shanty town" of Hollins. The fine Vicarage was demolished in 1925. In that year, local newspapers foretold the demolition of "the small and charming Dalehead Parish Church and the removal of the bodies from the graveyard."

For a time, buildings at Stocks Fold were used by the Fylde Water Board officials and contractors. Then the tractor and dragline levelled the village stores, the inn and smithy. Trees were grubbed up and burnt. The ravaged earth was prepared for flooding. The Filter House at Stocks was built in 1926 and the first supply pipe of water was in place three years later. Work on the overflow weir began in 1931. The great embankment and the valve tower cost £159,000.

The navvies, as recalled by J Heap, were footloose, staying for a few weeks, then moving to another job. They were big drinkers and most of them were totteringly drunk by eight o' clock in the evening. Mr Heap often asserted that the Water Board should have thanked Duttons Beer for the successful conclusion of the work; for without a steady supply of beer, brought in by special train, and retailed at fourpence a pint, the reservoir would not have been completed.

Jim Leeming, time-keeper and wages clerk, said there was no problem about recruiting labour: it was inexpensive and plentiful. Jim was born at Lower Brennand and his family moved to Eggberry, in the Upper Hodder Valley, in 1902. A further move took them to the heart of Stocks Fold and to a house next to Swales' Store—an area cleared and flooded by Fylde Water Board.

George Robinson, who got to know some of the navvies well, told me: "They were fairly straight. A spade was a spade. You knew what to make of 'em. They'd curse and do if they weren't suited."

The shriek of a railway steam whistle at 7am signified the start of the day's work. Work continued, with an hour's break at midday, until 5pm, the arrival of knocking-off time being indicated by the steam whistle. At the peak of the construction work, 1923-32, a navvy was paid a shilling an hour for a fifty-hour week, the time spread over five and a-half days. Theoretically, the average weekly pay was £2.10s. In a wet week, it was considerably less. A navvy was paid only for the time he was actually working.

As for the Fylde Water Board, the annual wages bill peaked in 1932, the year when the dam was completed. With an average rate per hour of 11½d, the grand total was £38,668. By the following year, it had fallen to £20,431.

Eleanor Sedgwick (nee Haigh), a teacher at Dalehead School in the 1920s, recalls: "We had a good life up there because the Fylde Water Board had a tennis club at Dalehead; it was really for their staff, but the locals could join if they wanted. The charge was ten shillings a year, so it was quite cheap."

Tennis was played not far from the old post office. "One of the Water Board workmen kept the court in order. Among the members were Mr and Mrs Cottam, the vicar and his wife, also the schoolmaster and his wife. And Jennie Cowking. We got some amusement when she arrived because she did not remain at her own side; she would be all over the place."

Hollins was the focal point for equipment used on the dam. Harry Cottam was heard to say: "Nothing is wasted at Hollins, other than the noise of the machinery!"

The power house, at the rear of Hollins village, was stated to be a fine example of up-to-date power installation, being equipped with three Beardmore petrol-driven engines of 160, 100 and 60 h.p. respectively. Electricity was generated for the electric cranes, air-compressors, stone-breakers and concrete-mixers. It also powered electrical fitments in the village. In charge of electrical production was an Engineer (R E Baley) and Chief Driver A Gillibrand had six assistants.

Much had already been written about the temporary village at Hollins, which—ten miles from the nearest community in any direction—had living accommodation in hutments for 330 workmen. Fifteen wooden huts were of the Army type, each hut presided over by a "housekeeper" who was responsible for the catering arrangements and the upkeep of the place.

The men slept in cubicles similar to ship bunks and shared a common living room. Following the annual visit of the constituent authorities in May, 1927, it was noted that "all the huts have trim flower gardens at the front and spacious vegetable gardens at the rear, the appearance of which speak eloquently of the leisure time spent in their cultivation."

Before Hollins was constructed, the men were transported each morning to the site of the dam in a special train—known as the Navvies Mail—and this train took them back to their lodgings in the evening. Ironically, when Hollins was proposed, it was necessary to build a small reservoir to supply the huts.

By 1925, when members of the constituent authorities had their annual tour of inspection, Hollins village was well established. A reporter from the *Blackpool Gazette* wrote: "This village has its main street and various streets which have been given the names of avenues; there are shops and stores, a hospital, electric light, water supply, sewerage scheme, refuse destructor and even a cinema theatre with a foyer.

"Children play about the residential parts of the little community when they are not at school, and the pure air of the hills has given them lovely complexions. Some of them have been born in the village."

A number of the workmen quartered at Hollins were Irish but some were "real owd English navvies. They followed public works all their life." A real navvy wore a fustian jacket, rough shirt and fustian trousers, complete with york-straps, leather belts, one round each leg. "York-straps kept the weight off your trousers and also out of t'muck." Most of the navvies wore clogs.

A party from Blackpool in the 1920s watched a party of navvies shovelling soil from the side of a hill to the trucks which carry it down to the spot where others tread it into the mixture required for filling up the dam. The visitors were impressed by "the machine-like regularity of the men. It was about five o'clock in the afternoon when we saw them, and they had been working nearly nine hours, which is their day's task." The men worked in gangs and had a friendly rivalry with regard to production.

Mechanisation had speeded up some processes. "The mechanical shovel, which is on view at some parts, is an example of how modern methods simplify labour. One man can shovel nine times the amount that another can achieve with the ordinary old-fashioned tool . . . The giant 'mechanical navvy' is another example of labour-saving on a vast scale. To see this monster literally eating out the side of a big cliff, three tons at a time, with clockwork regularity, is a contrast with the days when such tasks were painfully done at much greater cost and probably without the same efficiency."

It is recalled that the navvies used a toilet consisting of a trench screened by tin sheeting. The trench was about a yard deep. A post was driven in at each end and a plank put across as a seat. The trench was periodically filled in and when it was full the contraption was moved to another site. "Us lads, one dinner-time, thought we'd have a bit o' fun. Just sheer devilment. We sawed the underside of the plank some three quarters through. The navvies would go three and four at once. I think there were a curse on!"

A visitor to "the model village" noted "a well-stocked 'dry canteen' where everything within reason, from bully-beef to a suit of clothes, might be purchased at reasonable prices." In a "wet" canteen, the men quaffed "good English ale". Spirits were "tabooed". The profits the Board took from the canteen were utilised for the benefit of the men.

Hollins also had shops, cinema and a well-equipped hospital with a resident nurse. When the cinema was opened, local people were wide-eyed with wonder. "An observant stranger would probably have been puzzled by many twinkling lights on the hillsides (a sure sign in the country of some big 'do') all converging on the Works Railway down the Hodder Valley. The bearers of those lights were out to share a historic event—the opening ceremony for a cinema theatre."

The newspaper correspondent who penned those words "could scent something big in the air—something electrical." The Water Board had organised a free entertainment, with rail transport provided. "One train started at Tosside, conveying the people from that end and picking up passengers en route at Hesbert Junction, Dale Head, etc. Another train left Kenibus on the Bentham-road with passengers from the higher reaches of the Hodder, while the committee and staff were conveyed from Dale Head in a saloon car."

The new building impressed by its size—ninety feet by thirty feet with a floor space in the concert hall of seventy-five feet by twenty-eight feet, exclusive of the stage. "There is seating accommodation for three hundred people and the hall is equipped with a wireless installation."

The concert hall was to be used for dances, whist drives, concerts and social evenings. The newspaper correspondent, wholly impressed, wrote: "When one thinks of the navvies listening-in to concerts and music broadcast from different parts of England and abroad, one realises how times have changed since the old days when the 'blue-stockinged' brigade delved and dug without these advantages." He noted that the Board had provided "a large and well equipped canteen, electric light, football grounds, tennis courts, etc."

Eleanor Sedgwick was one of those who attended the cinema.

"We went every Thursday night and Mr Cottam had a rail-car we could use. I cannot remember how many it seated but it was always overloaded, the young men hanging on. I have known it have into the teens of passengers."

At the cinema "the locals sat in front and the navvies sat at the back. We had a three-piece band playing. When there was an interval we could get hot drinks, biscuits, chocolates and sweets. Now that Dalehead had no shop, it was an advantage to go to the wet canteen." Playing whist and dancing were two other social activities "and every now and again a concert party came to entertain us from Blackpool. And when they were coming, they ran a saloon car on the railway from Tosside right up to Dalehead."

A reporter of the *Blackpool Gazette* heard of the Hollins dance band, "on the approved Jack Hylton principle", and the dances which "are quite the most popular feature of the social round . . . From all round the countryside, the girls arrive on dance nights, looking about as much unlike the farm lasses of tradition as silk stockings and dainty clothes can make them. They come by bus, cycle, car or their own sturdy limbs, and romance has come with the waterworks into this lonely upland valley."

The hospital at Hollins had six beds. A qualified medical man was in daily attendance and minor accidents were treated immediately by Nurse Beeley, "the efficient wife of the storekeeper, B A Kinthorpe. They 'did their bit' in the Great War, the former being wounded, which necessitated his return to Blighty. He was sent to Haslingden Hospital for treatment and there came under the care of Nurse Beeley. The acquaintance ripened into a warmer feeling, and today there is no happier couple."

In 1924, Stocks football team "were worthy winners of the Gradwell Cup when they defeated Read by four goals to one. Anyone witnessing the first half of the game and then leaving would be amazed at the result for Stocks were greatly overplayed during the first forty-five minutes. Read, however, could not stay the course. . ." Midway in the second half, Jos Green (Stocks) and Rigby (Read) allowed their feelings to get the better of their discretion and the referee caught them fighting like urchins. He promptly sent the pair off the field."

Mr Cottam, the resident engineer, was chairman of Stocks FC and for the record, as they say, the Stocks contingent on that April day, 1924, consisted of J Wilkinson (capt), Joseph Green, R Atkinson, A Pinch, W B Blackwell, E Redfern, John Green, J Whittaker, J T Tivey, J B Driver, J Holden, G E Hurst, F Green.

Violet Cowgill, referring to the depot and sidings at Tosside, says: "As children we called it the Dump, for that's what it looked like. We saw it as we went to school at Tosside. Lengths of railway lines could be seen everywhere. Over thirteen miles of railway cost the Fylde Water Board £90,000."

In the summer of 1931, the famous petrol-driven railcar, which was at the disposal of Mr Cottam, the resident engineer, was involved in a serious accident. Mr Cottom was in charge at the time and the accident led to the death of his son Bryan. An account was given at the subsequent inquest, held at Blackburn Infirmary, the Coroner (F Thompson) sitting with a jury.

Mr Cottam stated that a light railway ran from his house to all parts of the Fylde waterworks. The railcar was used and he had frequently taken his sons for a ride. At 5pm on the day of the accident, he left in the car and the two boys were seated in the rear. Having passed through the works, he pulled up to speak to the Chief Engineer. Prior to stopping the car he had just passed over certain points, which his elder son had frequently worked. He had over-run the engine and reversed.

No sooner had he restarted than he saw the door of the car was open and heard a shout. He stopped immediately and found his younger son between the front and rear axles, badly hurt. (The boy had evidently left the car, thinking the points must be altered). The inquest verdict was "accidental death". The jury added a rider that in future children should not be allowed to ride on the engine.

For the interment, at St Andrew's, Slaidburn, the grave was lined with evergreens and roses. Employees of the Fylde Water Board at Stocks Reservoir were the bearers.

Fylde Water Board, concerned about the purity of the water, imposed such restrictions on farming in the area that the traditional way of life was no longer viable. In any case, most of the farmers were tenants. The owners had already cashed in the land and property over most of Dalehead. The farm folk had to disperse.

The Railcar crossing a temporary bridge.

Work on Stocks Reservoir was extended over nine years. When, in early July, 1932, Prince George pressed the electric button to put the reservoir into operation, a reporter of the *Advertiser and Times* sensed a dramatic moment. He wrote: "A great fountain of water rose in a foaming crescent from the foot of the huge embankment on which the Prince stood. Up and over, ever higher the waters sprang, then to fall with a steady roar into the stream below. . ."

The Fylde Water Board's "secret fears" of a water shortage were mentioned. The Board had been hurrying toward the completion of their Hodder scheme. "Hurrying but not scamping, for there can be no risks taken in a huge project such as this. Across the fertile valley that marked the source of the Hodder was built a mighty dam, joining the hills to form a basin for that great stretch of water, six miles in circumference and one hundred feet deep, destined to supply the Fylde's water needs for years to come."

There was sorrow at the loss of land and wonder at the scale of the reservoir work. "For nine years an army of workmen have been engaged in the task of transforming the countryside, and Tuesday's ceremony marked the completion of a £1,400,000 scheme begun in 1912 to lay for years the bogey of a water famine in the Fylde."

Prince George arrived at "the heart of the Bowland hills" to the applause of "excited villagers" and the sight of flag-bedecked buildings. "A steady stream of motors cars, each bearing an official blue pass, passed through Longridge, Little Bowland, Dunsop and Newton for two hours before the timed arrival of the Prince.

A block occurred at Dunsop when a Blackpool motor coach "jammed its undercarriage on the hump-backed bridge". The passengers were asked to dismount to lighten the load while, in cars immediately behind the bus, the Mayors of Preston and Lancaster fidgetted with frustration. When the motor coach cleared the bridge, a torrent of up to 50 vehicles was released.

Prince George left Knowsley at 10.20 with Lord Derby. Another car bore Lord Stanley, MP for the Fylde. At the site of the dam, the Prince was introduced to members of the Board, along with the clerk, John Hall, and the engineer, G F Atkinson. The supporting cast numbered at least one thousand people. It was a day of "warm sunshine and a tempering breeze".

The official account of that day is, as usual, one-sided. A local man says: "Them 'at worked on t'job were nowhere near; it was them big bugs from Blackpool who were in t'limelight." *The Manchester Guardian* made reference to "an army of workmen" who had been employed for seven years and to the cost of the scheme—£1,500,000..."A stock-rearing district has been converted into a huge lake."

The Prince (who wore in his buttonhole the red rose of Lancashire) said what was expected of him, making a special mention of Fylde Water Board's additional responsibility of providing water

FYLDE WATER BOARD

Inauguration of Hodder Supply

BY

H.R.H. The PRINCE GEORGE, K.G.,

Stocks Reservoir 5th July, 1932

PERMIT

TO VIEW THE CEREMONY

for the many visitors to the seaside towns. He had always regretted not being able to visit the Fylde district and to see Lancashire people enjoy themselves.

A local correspondent noted that the speech lasted "only a few minutes". Then came the "magic moment" when, stepping forward to a small table, "he pressed a silver button and immediately the Valley resounded to the shrill sound of hooters and engine whistles. The applause of the visitors was drowned." There followed a moment of silence. "Down below, a hundred feet away in the depths of the reservoir, the water began to rumble like the voice of an earthquake as it poured through the valve out into the valley below. As the valve slowly lifted, the rumbling grew louder. In a few moments the water began to pour through one of the huge bell pipes in a great spray of silvery white."

Councillor Robertson later mentioned that as the fountain of water appeared, Prince George had murmured "Beautiful". The Prince was led into the valve tower and was then taken to the far end of the embankment, where he unveiled a commemorative bronze plaque. In the filter house, officials had prepared glasses so that the Prince might taste the water, "but he passed on after examining the quality and it was left to his equerry to take the first sip."

After being entertained to lunch, the Prince boarded his car for a journey to Manchester, where he was to attend a performance of the Cotton Pageant. A thousand people dispersed. Dalehead was left in peace.

Tales at Random

In the 1920s, if you got £26 for a heifer it was a tip-top one.

Robin Waddington.

Two of my brothers were up at Court for poaching trout. My dad never got over that. He thought it was awful. He wouldn't know they were out, anyway...

A Tale of Raingill.

We used to be sent on errands to Tom and Lizzie Peel of Higher Stony Bank. Just slip up with this...And it would be a good mile. But you didn't hop on a bus then.

Margaret Jolly.

GOING to market was a major expedition in the days of horse transport. At the head of the dale, it was simplest to cross over to Bentham. Settle was patronised by those living to the east of the river. The majority of those who made the effort to attend a market made for Clitheroe with a horse-and-trap.

Those who drank a lot—who became "market fresh"—might depend on the horse's knowledge of the road to get home again. Tales were told of horses that stopped without command at every public house. During the absence of one man, some lads turned the horse round in the shafts and, emerging bleary-eyed from the inn, the owner was convinced the horse had thrown the trap over its head. "Farmers met their friends and one or two of them didn't mind if they had another pint or two." The weak-willed went "on the spree", living rough for days on end, drinking whenever they could.

Those who crossed Bowland Knotts and descended to Clapham

could catch a train to Lancaster or (if they wanted another tup for their stock) to Kirkby Stephen, completing the journey on the Settle-Carlisle railway. Norman Swindlehurst, of Keasden, remembered when a farmer walked to Clapham station, entrained for Settle, travelled to Kirkby Stephen, returned on the train with a new tup, left the train at Settle, walked the tup to Giggleswick, for Clapham, and eventually—wearily—dragged the tup up the hill road leading to Bowland Knotts.

Droving days are recalled by Robin Waddington. "They used to take the stuff from Dalehead to Hellifield. One of those drovers was Owd Mick, fra Settle—a reight big tall feller wi' ginger hair. He had summat wrong with his throat. They allus said he could drink twelve pints of beer while t'clock struck twelve."

Stephen Robinson had a cattle wagon. "He were t'best there were around. Stephen were good wi' t'stock. He could get 'em into t'wagon w'out any bother. He used to say: 'If you start wi' a stick, you only upset 'em'."

The folk at Lamb Hill and Catlow knew everyone on the Keasden side of the hill on account of the strag [stray] sheep which were knocking about. "They met each year at the sales and auction marts and so they kenned [recognised] farmers living as far down as Whitewell."

Tom Cowking remembers taking a sow to the boar in a cart. "When I got to the bottom of this hill, I looked round—and discovered the pig had gone. It had slipped out of the back. I had to go find this pig, bring it back and re-load it."

The Daleheaders of pre-reservoir times lacked the high mobility which is now provided by the private car. In the 'tween-war years, the motor bike was popular. Robin Waddington is one of those who remembers "t'owd belt driven things." He adds: "Th'owd joiner up at Tosside—Ziff Robinson, they called him—bought an old Douglas motor bike. I think he thought he'd getten the earth when he got 'od o' that. If you saw him on t'road, you couldn't help but start laughing. He had a gurt long coat on and a hard hat and he had a scarf over it. It was tied under his chin so that yon hat didn't blow away. He'd never look at you—just straight ahead."

Ziff had two apprentice joiners—Amrous [Ambrose] and George Briggs. Ziff's father was still alive. "Owd Steen [Stephen Robinson] was a bit cantankerous. He were also lame and he used to go about on a crutch. One day, he'd been laying the law down to Amrous reight. Amrous grabbed this crook and smashed it to smithereens."

Robin has clear memories of youthful walks from his farmhouse home across to th' Halsteads. "In them days, there were a lot o' footpaths. You were theer almost afore you set off. I used to walk to Tosside, then up what they call Bailey Lane to Hesbert Hall, Hindley Head and along a sort o' track that led straight to Halsteads. You were going straight nearly all t'way. "Th' Halsteads was just an ordinary farm but—by gum, tidy! You could have sat down for your meal anywhere in t'yard. (Then you'd go to another place and it'd be just as bad)."

Everything stopped for haymaking. The idea was to have some good hay ready for leading in the evening. That is when the midges were flying in clouds. A retired farmer recalls: "You could generally tell there was summat about when t'hoss started stamping." If it was "not quite hay", a footcock was made, using the rake to twist over a piece of grass. This was "brokken out" next day. Two footcocks equalled one hub, "one at t'top of t'other . . . It had to be hubbed up or it wasn't good hay." This farmer did not remember pikes [mini-stacks] being made when he was young. "They came later."

Vic Robinson, one of a family long settled at Stephen Park, tells of the self-reliant days. When his father went to Clitheroe—once a year, at the time of the horse sales—mother went with him and spent the day at the home of a cousin, John Parkinson and his wife. He was headmaster of St James's School. The journeys to and from Clitheroe were by horse and trap. "If it was cold weather, it was a cold drive."

Vic's father's mind was on nothing else but horses. "They didn't pay the rent. That was paid by sheep. He hadn't any interest in sheep. It was horses every time. They had to have the best of hay. They had to have the best of everything. But they didn't always get it. I saw to that!"

Back on the farm, mother fed a large family and helpers at a table made from ash which had grown in Park Wood. "The table was three yards long and a yard wide; it had three drawers. There was a single white tablecloth, to be used on special occasions. When our stuff was sold up, a man called Hird, who was living at Skirden Hall, near Tosside, bought the table; he sawed it into two to get it out of the building.

The Robinsons of Stephen Park and the Cowkings of New Close were great friends. In the days when entertainment was home-made, they would get together for a sing-song at the piano, rendering the latest songs, such as *Moonlight and Roses*. Normally, there was little spare time.

Corn was grown and milled on the premises for oatmeal, which was kept in an oak kist [box] measuring twelve feet by eight feet and with a height of six feet. "It hadn't a nail in it, just wooden pegs. They used to fill that kist with oatmeal. Our womenfolk played pop about having this in a bedroom; they couldn't get round it to clean the room."

Mother made oatcake on a "backstone", which was heated by a fire. She would mix the oatmeal the day before it was needed and it was left in a big dish. "Then she had a measure, sufficient for one oatcake. The long, thin cakes were hung over a clothes line near the fire to dry. When they had set [gone hard] they looked like wash-leathers. You could have oatcake which way you liked—with butter or treacle or porridge. We enjoyed it."

The Daleheaders were dependent for their groceries on the travellers of Clitheroe or Settle-based firms. "If they couldn't get, they brought it so far and let us know." The Robinsons bought meat from Pearson Rumney of Long Preston and Howards of Newton, though little was required because the farmyard swarmed with chickens, ducks, even geese (though eating a goose was usually a Christmas treat).

Shepherd and Walker were noted chemists who supplied medicines for such complaints as "wooden tongue" in cattle or provided derris powder to cope with attacks on stock by the warble fly. They also advertised themselves as "grocers and oil merchants". In the 1920s, Jack Walker was the traveller who visited farms at Dalehead. Originally he cycled on his rounds and then he was provided with an American type of car called an Overland. The orders he collected were delivered within a few days by Billy Fletcher, originally using a horse and two wheeled cart and eventually a motor vehicle.

Groceries were ordered in bulk—for example, flour was delivered by the sackful—and the coffee (2s.8d per lb) was ground at the last moment. As the shop staff turned the large wheel of the grinding machine, Billy Fletcher would be stamping his feet impatiently outside, anxious to be off on his rounds.

These took in Clough Hall and Halsteads. For the last stage of the journey to Halsteads, Billy put the ordered goods in a wheelbarrow. The occupants of such a remote farm hung on to a traveller, anxious to know all that was going on in the outer world.

In 1926, Shepherd and Walker invested in a Willys Knight Overland van, of USA origin though it was assembled at Trafford Park in Manchester. The ever-cheerful Billy Fletcher was fond of saying that the maintenance costs of the Overland van over six years totalled thirty shillings. It had needed a new set of plugs. When Billy took one of the young Walkers on his rounds as a special treat during the summer holiday, his passenger was to remember the rutted state of the road between Long Preston and Tosside, which was being traversed by huge traction engines transporting equipment to the reservoir works.

Billy would give a fascinating description of what was seen, his most arresting story being that of the removal of bodies from the churchyard at dead of night and their interment in the grounds of the new mortuary chapel.

Vic has special memories of the harvests of the summer—of making hay and cutting turf [peat]. At Stephen Park, haytime was mechanised to the extent of a two-horse mowing machine, strawing machine and side delivery. Young horses, 'schooled' in the chain harrow, now took their share of hard work. If the weather was hot, mowing began in the early morning. "You hadn't to sweat a horse too hard."

Mother laid in a stock of liquid refreshment. For the lads, it was ginger beer in a niner [nine gallon cask] and for the Irishmen it was beer in a big barrel. "That barrel was delivered from Clitheroe by horse and flat cart. To me the barrel stank. I couldn't do with the smell of beer but the Irishmen would not work without they got it."

Mother made Stewart's Stout, also nettle beer. Vic had a special liking for blackcurrant tea. It was easily made, in a pint pot. A spoonful of blackcurrant jam was mixed with a little warm water and the pot was filled up with cold water.

Stephen Park had eighty acres of meadowland and each year 40 cartloads of turf were transported to the farm as fuel. "When the first coal strike was on, Mr Procter [the landlord] said anyone who could get turf would be allowed to take it from the Stephen Park patch on Park Moss, where there were tons of it, in pits a good five feet deep.

"When you first cut turf it was like black butter. It was terrible stuff to move because your fingers went through it. Then you got t'dodge off and you were not rough with it as you lifted it. One turf was reared against another, making four in a group, to catch the wind and sunshine. You had to keep the cattle and sheep off or they'd knock over the heaps and make a heck of a mess."

When the turves were somewhat dry, they were built into a conical heap, leaving gaps and creating a honeycomb effect, allowing the wind to blow through and completing the drying process. Then a turf was as hard as a piece of coal. "You could have walled with it!" In contrast was the turf lifted from a spot in the front meadow at Stephen Park. "This was more like pressed sticks. It had not rotted down the same as it had on Park Moss."

Stephen Park had a peat-house. The turves were transported to it using an ordinary cart with special "shilvings". Turf and wood from toppled trees kept the home fires burning the year through. The main fire was in the kitchen, the fireplace being made of iron, with a boiler at one side and an oven at the other. Vic remembers a small plate bearing the name and address of the supplier—Manby's of Skipton.

The relentless programme of hard work was relieved by Sports Day, held in Gamble Fold, just opposite the School, the races being run for monetary prizes. "Womenfolk made a real tea—sandwiches, cakes, trifles—in the schoolroom." When Vic left school and started work at home, "I was not paid a penny by my Dad. I'd only what I got off my Mother. She was very good-hearted."

Violet Cowgill recalls hot days when a basin of butter was placed beside the beck near Bridge House to keep the butter firm. Children were forbidden to go near the cliff-edge above the Hodder which is now the western side of the island in the reservoir.

The stepping stones on the Hodder near Grange Hall were too widely separated for the comfort of children. Violet says: "It wanted nerve to cross that river with Clarice Cowking."

She also tells a story of Cousin Ted's motor bike which he kept in a boarded-off section of the shippon. When he took to the road, he paid 1s.3d a gallon for fuel and had a companion, a "cheerful little black bitch he called Jet. My father gave it to him as a puppy and Ted trained it.

"For long journeys on the motor bike, he made a sturdy wooden box and fixed it on the pillion seat for Jet to sit in. She wasn't fastened in and she never jumped out."

As a child, Violet Cowgill walked with a Shire mare and cartload of hay up a local brow. When father decided the horse should have a rest, Violet's job was to "scotch" the wheels of wood or stone to prevent the cart from running back.

Once, when the Slaidburn and Dale Head Whit Monday Sports were held, a small pig was released. It would become the property of whoever caught it. Maisie Wharton ran after it until she almost dropped, but when the pig was exhausted it was left to Marjorie Simpson to grab it.

Ted Robinson, of Stephen Park, recalled to Violet Cowgill how, when the reservoir was complete, his father let the young men of the area use a redundant granary as their meeting place. George Thompson remembers the little joiners' shop at Stocks Fold. When the Fylde Water Board took over, they ran a railway line here to collect sleepers made at the old shop. The circular saw was driven by a paraffin engine. "The engine went chuff, chuff, chuff, then CHUFF—a right big one! The exhaust came up at t'back of t'building. We used to put our hats on and they were blown sky-high. One lad grabbed someone else's cap, put it on the exhaust and stuck to it."

Everyone recalls schooldays at Dalehead, when old-time

teachers inflicted corporal punishment on wrong-doers, even those children who had long walks through the fields and arrived a few minutes later. "If we'd been late a time or two, there'd come a day when we came in at the door to find the cane was at the back of our legs. Another time, a table was moved and a trapdoor opened. We had to spend a bit o' time underground. A teacher would be done [prosecuted] now for doing things like that."

Doris Wells smiles at the recollection of paper chases organised during the dinnertime break at Dalehead School. "We'd walked three miles to school and we would walk three miles back home again—and at mid-day we chased each other for miles." Tom Lodge, one of a large family living at Tenters, started school at Dalehead when he was four years old. He walked with his brother John, who was five. The way to school lay entirely through fields.

Among Tom's recollections of those days are the big stacks of peat at the house-ends. "There was a peat-house at Tenters. You could back a horse and cart to where you could tip the peats under cover. The Tenters peat came from Jonathan Heights. It was very near our farm. Each summer, families made their way to the workings."

The first job was to take off the surface material and throw it into the bottom. A channel was left to allow the water to drain. The top was removed because it was rubbish. The best of the peat was down below. "A peat-digger went down till it was just like cutting butter. Then you were away. . . I've wheeled turf out with a barrow and helped to set 'em up. They used to put a bit more peat on my barrow because I was a bit bigger than the others."

Vic Robinson tells of cutting peat which was nearly as hard as coal and which kept the fires at Stephen Park burning the year through.

Dalehead had a good number of characters. Vic's father used to relate how his mother—Nanna Robinson of Park—"wore the breeches". Her word was law. "The rhubarb bed covered almost an acre because there were six men turning in every meal-time; they took some catering for. One time they had so much rhubarb they were fair stalled of it and so a man took a scythe and mew [mowed] the lot.

"Nanna, unperturbed, collected up the sticks of rhubarb into bundles, dried them out and continued to serve the stuff at every meal."

Appendices

1 — Some of those employed at Dalehead

ATKINSON, G F — The Board's Engineer
COTTAM, JOHN — Resident Engineer
GIBSON, JACK — Engine Driver
HEAP, J — Chief Clerk
PORTER, JACK — Engine Driver
LEEMING, JIM — Time-keeper and Wages Clerk
WALKER, MERRY — Engine Driver

2 — Cost of Constructing the Reservoir

Up to 1920 — £22,000. 1921 — £61,968. 1922 — £47,468.
1923 — £55,978. 1924 — £49,027. 1925 — £68,416.
1926 — £85,175. 1927 — £59,860. 1928 — £52,428.
1929 — £54,540. 1930 — £61,391. 1931 — £45,447.
1932 — £50,770.

3 — Some of the Farms at the Time of the 1861 Census (Also given are the acreage and names of farmers)

Brown Hill (34 acres) — John Carr
Dob Dale (26) — Stephen Dawson
North Field (56) — Ambrose Grimshaw
Clough Hill (112) — Pheanby Cort
Tenters (94) — Ann Hodgson
Bottoms (107) — William Harrison
Hindley Head (100) — Stephen Harrison
Hesbert Hall (three farms)
  (114) Richard Taylor
  (100) Richard Wooler
  (160) Stephen Wooler
Long Dyke (62) — Mary Common
Sandy Dyke (34) — Henry Robinson
Stephen Park (355) — Stephen Robinson
Cocklick House (70) — William Wood
Greenfold (two farms)
  (70) — William Slinger
  (50) — George Cort
Hammerton Hall (120) — John Brennand
Grange Hall (160) — Thomas Cowking
Hollins (two farms)
  (80) — John Hanson
  (150) — William Hanson
New Close (163) — James Kinder
Swinshaw (184) — William Blackburn
Higher Croft House (30) — George Spencer
Lower Croft House (70) — Thomas Taylor Robinson
Lower Birch Hill (54) — Thomas Blackburn
Cocklick End (48) — William Harrison
Old Ing (52) Benjamin Butler
Higher Halsteads (280) — John T Harrison
Lower Halsteads (128) — John Butler

Fair Hill (464) — Elizabeth Dichoner
Higher Clough (106) — Bryan Blackwell
Lower Clough (34) — William Oldfield
New House (726) — Anthony Nelson
Chapel House (173) — William Hargreaves
Collyholme (177) — Peggy Parker
Catlow (787) — Thomas Frankland
Whitehill House (38) — Richard Coates

4 — Members of the Commission who considered the ecclesiastical position of Dalehead and who met in Dalehead School:

Lewis George Dibdin, barrister-at-law, appointed by the Ecclesiastical Commissioners;
the Rev Canon Ackerley, Rector of Carleton-in-Craven, representing the Bishop;
Col J W R Parker, of Browsholme Hall, Clitheroe, representing the patron and Parochial Church Council of Dalehead;
Col Charles Julius Hirst, of Townhead, Slaidburn, representing the patron and Parochial Church Council of the Parish of Slaidburn;
and H C Frankish, of the School House, Tosside, representing the patron and Parochial Church Council of the Parish of Tosside.

5 — The family of William Carr (1854—1936) and Elizabeth Ann, nee Robinson (1856—1939), who farmed Fair Hill from 1880 until 1910. All appeared on a photograph taken in 1909. It was the only time they had been at home together since childhood.

Mary born July 17, 1878; Henry born Sept 7, 1879; Thomas born Sept 7, 1879; Eunice born Jan 4, 1881; Isabel born Mar 23, 1882; Heber born Aug 24, 1883; John born July 2, 1885; Ruth born Jan 16, 1887; Bridget Ellen born Aug 22, 1888; Elizabeth born Dec 28, 1889; Allan born Sept 13, 1891; Jane born Apl 10, 1893; William born Oct 6, 1895; Lois born July 22, 1901.